LIFE IN THE PACIFIC
FIFTY YEARS

£5

al

106 Southborough Rd

Bromley - Kent

VIEW OF NASOVA, FIJI
By F. C. Gordon Cumming.

LIFE IN THE PACIFIC
FIFTY YEARS AGO

BY
ALFRED P. MAUDSLAY

With an Introduction by
T. A. JOYCE

AND 2 PLATES AND A MAP

LONDON
GEORGE ROUTLEDGE & SONS LTD.
BROADWAY HOUSE: 68-74 CARTER LANE, E.C.
1930

PRINTED IN GREAT BRITAIN BY
M. F. ROBINSON & CO. LTD., AT THE LIBRARY PRESS, LOWESTOFT

INTRODUCTION

It is a great compliment to be invited to write a foreword to the personal reminiscences of a man who has performed such services to the State, both in the Proconsular and Archæological fields, as Alfred Maudslay. But it is not an easy task. If I wrote as I think, Maudslay would apply a severe censorship. All who have had the great privilege of knowing Maudslay personally, and his life history, will understand the position, and will know that I am writing with a muzzled pen. The careful reader will discover for himself that what Maudslay has left unsaid provides an example of eloquent silence. We find him stressing the fact that, in his schooldays, he was a dunce at languages. But shortly after his arrival in the Pacific he is delivering speeches in the Fijian tongue. No one could accuse Maudslay of lack of capacity ; the fact is that, from his earliest days, he had the direct mind of the man of action, which refused to apply itself to the study of a subject for which he could see no practical use.

His public school experience, of which he writes half-humourously and half-affectionately, gave him exactly that training which enabled him to deal successfully with primitive peoples. That training was acquired, not in the class-room, but from the peculiar atmosphere which pervaded (and I still hope pervades) all great British Public Schools. There is nothing more akin to a primitive social complex than a British Public School, regarded as a community outside the class-room. I have always felt that the great success of our youthful Empire-builders is due to this particular fact. Maudslay's narrative provides a very good instance, to which he alludes so lightly that it might well escape notice. I refer to the partition of Samoa. England, Germany and the United States were each trying to obtain the cession of the islands. The young Maudslay obtained the concession from the paramount chiefs for this country by his own personal influence and tact, only to find that an agreement had been concluded by the home cabinets which robbed him of a great diplomatic achievement.

I can say no more on this subject, or I shall be censored by the author, so I will turn critic. Maudslay's reminiscences only include his experiences in the Pacific. Why stop there? Maudslay's great contribution to science resulted from seven expeditions which he made to Central America between 1881 and 1894. His excavations, and the moulds which he made from the Early Maya monuments, not only provided the National Museum with a series of casts and original sculptures which are unique, but also furnished the material on which the elucidation of the hieroglyphic script of the Maya is based.

With regard to these field researches I can write with some authority, because I, too, have had experience in the Central American Bush, supported by all the conveniences provided by modern transport and food-supply. These were not available to Maudslay. My complaint is that he has not finished his memoirs, and that the personal account of his experiences in Central America is not told. His scientific results were published in the series *Biologia Centrali-Americana :* and a shorter account in a book entitled *A Glimpse of Guatemala*. But what we want is a personal record of those years in Central America from the pen of the pioneer of Central American Archæology. There is no English term. I can only say *Le Maître*.

T. A. JOYCE

British Museum.

CONTENTS

LIFE IN THE PACIFIC FIFTY YEARS AGO

CHAPTER I

SCHOOL AT HARROW

I was born on the 18th March, 1850, at Lower Norwood Lodge, and there we lived until the place was sold and my father and mother moved to 21 Hyde Park Square.

One of my earliest recollections is being taken by my nurse to the garden of the Convent in Upper Norwood to watch the carriages go by to the opening of the Crystal Palace. When as children we were sent to the seaside in the summer (where my father used to visit us in his yacht) our nearest railway station was Croydon, about seven miles distant.

I well remember the old country inn near the Norwood Cemetery, which stood back from the road with a row of pollarded lime-trees in front of it and a big swinging signboard, and I always ran past it fast, because the nursemaid told me the new railroad was coming through there, and I thought it might come dashing through at any moment.

We were at Folkestone in September, 1855, and

1

I can vividly remember my father, who could not walk, excitedly working his wheeled chair along the Lees and waving over his head a copy of the *Times* announcing the fall of Sebastopol.

When I was between the ages of ten and eleven I was sent to a boarding school at Tunbridge Wells. Unfortunately it was a school living on its past reputation : the founder was still alive, but he had turned over the school to his son, a good-natured, indolent parson with a drunken wife. The school hours were long, but we learnt nothing, and I spent most of the time reading novels half-hidden under the desk. Luckily we were left quite free in play-time, and had the common in front of us for games, and on whole holidays often went far afield on our rambles ; once I walked with another small boy to Tonbridge, and thence to Penshurst, because I wanted to go over Penshurst Place, and home by Speldhurst, where I unexpectedly found the tomb of my great-aunt in the churchyard. It was about a twenty-mile walk, and I was rather stiff the next day.

In 1861 my father, who had been an invalid for some years, died.

After Easter, 1863, I was sent to Harrow. At the entrance examination I was placed last but one in the school, for strange to say there was found one boy who knew less than I did. Most of one's time in school was taken up in writing nonsense Latin verses ; " the sense however was no great matter ", indeed it was none, and the greatest crime one could commit was a false quantity. It was simply a puzzle worked out with a Latin dictionary and a gradus. In the next higher forms, when we were supposed to know the difference between a dactyl and a spondee, we were promoted to do verses from a book with copious notes to assist us; and in the shell and lower fifth form, which I finally attained, we were sometimes given a subject on which to write twenty Latin verses. I seldom or never had a set of Latin verses passed, even with the help which was often afforded me by my schoolfellows; but I did perpetrate eight or ten lines of an invocation to the muse, which was useful on several occasions, with sufficient intervals of time between, and suited any subject. This, even after corrections by more than one master, was such bad Latin that no one could say it was not my own. Latin verses did indeed seem to be considered the principal means of education.

Dr Henry Montague Butler had been headmaster for three years when I entered the school. He was a young man, and was not popular with the boys. One particular reason was that he had ordered our trouser pockets to be sewn up! Someone, I believe, had written a letter to a newspaper to say that he had visited Harrow, and had seen the boys slouching about, all round-shouldered, with books under their arms, and hands in their trouser-pockets. If one was carrying books under one's arm, it was natural to put one's hand into one's trouser-pocket to support them (there were no coat-pockets, as we wore either jackets or tail-coats). But the edict went forth, and we were all furious. I well remember the fire of chaff we were subjected to from the Eton boys at Lord's that year.

By the way, this was the last year that what was called " chaff " at Lord's was allowed. It had often degenerated into personal abuse, shouted by youthful lungs—a good deal directed that year against the personal appearance of that great cricketer, I. D. Walker, who was our Captain. Both sides were equally to blame. From the moment the bowler took the ball into his hand there were shouts of Bub-Bub-Bub Bowled ! Every failure to field a ball was ironically cheered, and it was a great relief when the M.C.C. forbade everything but legitimate applause.

As I got slowly up the school, the form I was in was always far ahead of me in classics, and I practically left them alone and scraped together a few marks in other subjects. But these subjects were very few ; there was no English history, no geography, and very little time was devoted to Roman and Greek history, and I remember that if one was half asleep in class, and a question was put to you, it was safest to take a shot and answer, " A river in Asia Minor ", or " An island in the Ægean Sea". I don't think I ever successfully got through a ' repetition ' (which was mostly twenty lines of Virgil or an ode of Horace), for I could not commit to memory lines I could not understand. I was usually told to sit down and write it out so many times. When I got into Bowen's form, he saw what was the matter, and lent me books to read. By the time I was in dear old Farrer's form I had worked out a system. On Sunday we were given three or four chapters of the Old Testament to read, and a class was held in the afternoon. More than half the boys would read the headings of the chapters, skim the rest, and trust to luck. I used to read the chapters carefully, go to the Vaughan Library, look up the names in the Dictionary of the Bible, and the places in Stanley's *Sinai and Palestine;* and I would answer a dozen questions to the ordinary good boy's four or five. That meant ten marks for each question, and I was well started for the week. Next morning it was Greek Testament; I would read the English version and trust to luck for the rest. In any subject in English I would try and get marks. On Thursday, for example, we were given a subject for a short essay, or more often twenty lines of rhyming verse as an evening exercise. It never gave me any trouble to write twenty lines of execrable doggerel but it rhymed and scanned, and I used to get nearly full marks, and I wrote most of the exercises for the boys in the form who were in my house. It is astonishing the utter inability of some boys to rhyme, and often there is no sense of rhythm. I have actually seen boys take the school hymn-book, cover up all but the rhymes at the end of the lines and write their English verses up to those rhymes.

Farrer was a bad master in one respect, for he

had pet good boys and pet bad boys. I was one of the latter, and he used to tap me on the head with his long pointing rod and call me " a barren tree " and " an arid desert ", with plentiful rolling of the r's. I remember, when we had been reading the story of the choice of Hercules in Xenophon's *Memorabilia*, that we were told to write thirty lines of verse on the subject as an evening exercise, and a certain noble lord, who usually sat near me at the bottom of the form, gave up the following as his exercise—

> " Hercules went for a walk
> and met virtue and vice
> looking very nice "

and when remonstrated with said, " Please, sir, I could not help it, the words would not come ".

Saturday was my busy day, for the evening exercise was a map. This did not mean any instruction in map-drawing, it only meant that we had a map to copy out of the school atlas, and one bought from Polly Arnold a twopenny bit of cardboard and a paint-brush and a couple of paints.

If the subject was given out early enough, I generally got my map done the day before. Then it would be " Be a good fellow and put in my outsiders and lats. and longs ". Then another would want his mountains put in, and I drew caterpillars across the card more or less in position. Another wanted his tints put on, or his rivers inked, and as I did not make them run up-hill they were quite satisfactory. So I was generally kept busy all the evening.

6

In the lower school, if any particularly good exercise was sent in to a form master the author was " sent up " with it to the headmaster. I only twice had this honour conferred on me, once for an English epitaph on Socrates, which I cannot remember anything about, and the other time for a map of Harrow to be done entirely out of our own heads, and we were put on our honour not to look at any printed map or plan. I believe mine was really quite a creditable performance.

On the other hand, we were more often " sent up " to the headmaster for misbehaviour or idleness, and sometimes got a swishing. I was only swished once, my principal offence being falling asleep at evening chapel. The sermons in the morning were often interesting, for a clerical master had only to preach once or twice in a term, but Butler preached every Sunday evening, and something in his voice inevitably sent me to sleep, and perhaps I snored.

Farrer about this time gave one of the Friday evening lectures at the Royal Institution, criticizing the prevalent system of education, and spoke of the ordinary intelligent boy who gained little by it, and he afterwards told my mother that he had me in mind.

So I left Harrow unable to read the simplest passages of a Latin or Greek author.

I am not inveighing against a classical education. I believe there is none better if a boy is well grounded, and if when he knows something of the language the subjects are made interesting to him, and he has any literary taste; but I had no grounding whatever.

As I was writing this, I saw in a newspaper that Mr Baldwin had gone to Harrow on Speech Day. I can remember a Speech Day when another Prime Minister, Lord Palmerston, was expected, but failed to appear at the time appointed. After the visitors had gone up to the Speech Room and the speeches had begun, I happened to be standing alone by the school gate when Lord Palmerston rode up, dismounted, gave his horse to his groom, and looked at his watch and said, " One hour from Hyde Park Corner ". Then he took a little looking-glass and a brush from his coat-pocket, brushed up his whiskers, and trotted up the steps to the Speech Room.

I was told afterwards that he was delighted because one of the speeches chosen for recitation was his speech on the affair of the Lorcha " Arrow ", which ended with the words " Romanus Civis Sum ".

The Grove was certainly the roughest house in Harrow. The house-master, The Reverend Thomas Steele, commonly known as Tommy, seldom came near us except to read prayers before supper, and we were left to the tender mercies of the housekeeper, Mrs Harding, commonly known as Dingo. The head of the house was the only boy who had a room to himself. There were four rooms with five beds in each, no studies; only one room with four beds had studies, the others three and two beds. It was the rule of the strongest; the head boy had little or no influence. In the winter, when we were

shut in from six until lights out at ten (with
sometimes an hour of " Pupil room " in the Hall for
the lower boys, when Tommy would be present), we
were left to ourselves. Word would go out from
the strongest room that after supper it would be
boxing to-night, or jumping, or high-cock, and
we met in the biggest room and started our games.
High-cock was a sort of leapfrog. One boy was
told to bend down against the wall and " make a
back " ; the next boy jumped on his back, and
then the boys of each side went on fitting in and
piling up, until the heap gave way, or the last boy
jumped right to the top and cried out some words
that I have forgotten. Of course the biggest boys
came last, and it was a severe strain on the boys
underneath ; one night one of them broke a blood
vessel, and then the game was stopped.

With boxing we were told off in couples according
to size, and practically had to fight it out with gloves.
This I did not much mind, as I was good with the
gloves for my size. Other nights it was high jumping. Even on other nights, when there were no games,
with five boys in one room and others running in
and out of it, it can easily be imagined that there
was little chance of quiet work. When lights were
out, we always kept a hidden supply of candles,
so as to finish up any necessary work, or more often
to write " lines " which had been given as punishment. We often read in bed ; the usual arrangement
was to take two magnum bonum pens, from which
the nibs had been broken off, leaving sharp points

which could easily be driven into the wooden sides of the box in which the bed swung back when shut up in the daytime. On these two pens it was easy to fix a candle, and they could be hastily removed if necessary, for Tommy sometimes came round about midnight. One night, Hyder, the boy who had the bed next to me, was sitting up at the table writing " lines " when we heard Tommy's footstep on the stairs; the light was out, and Hyder was in bed and asleep in a second. Tommy came quietly in, with a candle in his hand, looked round our beds until he came to Hyder. " Hyder, Hyder ", he said, " we don't go to bed in our spectacles." The unfortunate Hyder was short-sighted. Tommy pulled down the bedclothes, and alas, Hyder had failed to undress !

It was an old and mostly wooden house, and how we escaped a conflagration is a wonder.

We were not too well fed, and as long as pocketmoney held out we supplemented the fare in various ways, buying cutlets or sausages from the tuckshops for breakfast, which we had to carry home on plates. We had to pass by the house of Middlemas, a mathematical master, on the way to the Grove, and his study overlooked the street, and the old curmudgeon objected to our carrying plates, and punished us if we did so. So we had to carry hot cutlets, etc., wrapped up in greased paper. When I was a small boy, and fagging for the head of the house, this was my daily duty. Fagging, though sometimes a nuisance, was really no hardship. We could generally buy surreptitious bottles of Bass from Old Troke the butler. We had a way of getting out of the house after lock-up, but it was hardly ever used. It was done by taking out the screws from one of the bars in the Hall window and strapping the loose bar to a fixed one, when there was just room to squeeze through and drop down to the ground. When the strap was released the bar went back in place. However, in the summer we sometimes used this means of escape when starting very early on Sunday mornings on bird's-nesting expeditions, getting back in time for chapel.

A feat often talked about, but only once accomplished I think, in my time, was to run to the Thames and see the University Boat Race. This could only be done when the race was rowed very early, as it often was in those days. I remember one boy in our house who attempted it being brought back in a state of utter collapse. I forget what excuse he made to the authorities.

Another thing it was tempting to do, because it was strictly prohibited, was to go to the Harrow Races, which were held a mile or two from the foot of the hill. This, however, I was determined to do, and with two boys from another house arranged our plans. I hired a little rough pony-cart, which was to meet us at the bottom of the hill. We were to be disguised as three local ragamuffins, and were to send our coats and hats, etc., to the care of the owner of the pony-trap. When we changed our clothes in a shed, it was decided that my coat was too respectable, so I borrowed the coat from the boy who had brought the trap. One watch was taken with no chain, and this watch Stephenson put loose in his trousers pocket. We got to the course all right, and as we all knew the native lingo, there was little chance of detection. I got some coppers from a schoolfellow for holding his horse. He was got up with a false moustache and swagger clothes and was driving a dog-cart, and he never recognized me. After a time I noticed we were followed by the police, and were finally all three arrested on the charge of stealing a watch. Then they searched us, and the loose watch was found in Stephenson's pocket, and he could neither tell the name of the maker nor the number on the watch, when asked. I had not dared to put my hands into the pockets of the coat I had borrowed, but when they were turned out they produced several curious articles which I could not account for. So I was led off with the Bobby's hand on my collar. For a time we kept up our disguise, but when I saw the matter was serious, for the owner of the lost watch was insistent that we had taken it, I asked to see the Superintendent, and told him that we were three Harrow boys out on a spree. He first of all told me " that wouldn't do ", but after I had talked to him in my natural voice and answered questions about whose house I was in, he began to have doubts ; but it was some time before I could convince him, and then he sent us back in charge of a mounted policeman.

Stephenson and Trotter ran up the hill and just got in time to answer their names. It took longer changing my borrowed coat, but I had no jacket, only the coat that had been condemned as too respectable. However, when, quite out of breath, I reached the School yard, one sympathetic boy lent me his jacket and another brought me a basin and towel to wash my face; and I ran up the steps into the fourth form room, where I had been marked as absent; but dear old John Smith had been calling Bill, and he patted me on the shoulder, and ticked off the mark in the Bill Book against my name and asked no questions.

There was a draggletail old charwoman who came to clean out our rooms once or twice a week, and I used to make love to her, because she would bring me flowers from her cottage garden. I was in a smaller room then with only three beds in it, and we used to try and keep it tidy. When next the old girl came, she nodded her head mysteriously and whispered, " I know all about it. I know where you've been. My son's a policeman, and 'twas him as arrested you ".

Sometimes after Bill there was the excitement of a fight, and directly this news went round we all crowded along the wall of the school yard overlooking the milling ground, or formed a ring on the ground itself. Fighting was a recognized institution and no master interfered. Everything was done in order; seconds were chosen by the combatants, and Sam Hoare, the school custos, brought basins and a sponge. The biggest fight I saw was between Marjoribanks, and Graham, both strapping big boys. Graham had the longer reach and the most science, but Marjoribanks fought very pluckily and took his punishment well, until he was completely exhausted and his seconds threw up the sponge. We in the Grove settled our differences in a private milling ground in the Grove, as we did not think our domestic squabbles should be made public.

Towards the end of my time Angelo's people added instruction in boxing to the lessons they already gave in fencing, if one liked to pay for it, and it was remarkable how fights in the milling ground decreased ; perhaps we knew too much of an opponent's quality.

I was not a strong boy, frequently catching heavy colds and with a chronic cough ; and going out to school unfed on winter mornings and not returning to breakfast until nine did not improve matters, so I was taken to Dr Quain to be overhauled. He said no football or cricket, and rum and milk every morning before I went out. The rum and milk was put by my bedside every night, and I must say this for my schoolfellows, they never played tricks with it, and I think it was my salvation. In my last term things improved a bit, and hot bread and milk was served in the hall for any boys who chose to take it, but it was rather a scramble.

In spite of orders I used to play rackets, and I won the house hurdle race and was only just beaten for the school hurdles. I also won the Elvington

Challenge Cup for the School high jump, and I shot for the school at Wimbledon in the team that won the Ashburton Shield.

The Grove was a delightful bit of wild woodland, and I spent a good deal of my time there in summer. The other boys seldom came there except to skate on the pond in winter or for bird's-nesting in the spring. I used to catch perch in the Grove pond and get the cook to cook them for my tea. I never knew such a place for birds ; nightingales swarmed, and as the trees came right up to our windows, I have heard a good deal of strong language used when the chorus kept some boys awake.

As a small boy I had joined the Choir of ten boys who sat in the organ loft of the Chapel. There was no instruction, and it was a very poor business ; we were rather looked down upon by the other boys. During my last year Farmer became organist, and effected a complete revolution. He started house singing for an hour every week in the winter evenings ; it caught on at once, and " Harrow Songs " written by Bowen and composed by Farmer are now known all over the world.

I think I came to Harrow at the end of the old régime, and things began to move just before I left. A science master was appointed, and some of the hours that used to be devoted to Latin verses were given up to history. When I visited the school a few years ago, I hardly knew my old house : all the rooms were divided up into single rooms or double rooms with studies. There was an efficient nurse in charge instead of old Dingo, and she told me the boys were not allowed to wander about from room to room after lock-up.

All these changes are, I am sure, for the better, but I don't for a moment regret my own experience there, although I acquired little book learning, and passed through some hard times in the house.

CHAPTER II

CAMBRIDGE

On leaving Harrow I went to Mr Rhodes, a Tutor at Bonchurch in the Isle of Wight. There were five or six boys ; those I remember were Bruce, afterwards Lord Aberdare, and Powell, later on a Professor of Modern History at Oxford. It was a pleasant life and we did not do much work, but bathed and rambled about the country.

Mrs Rhodes was an agreeable woman, a daughter of Professor Ferrier and granddaughter of Professor Wilson of the *Noctes Ambrosianæ*. Mrs Ferrier used often to stay with us, and I wish I could remember all the stories she told me about Edinburgh Society in her youth.

Those Ambrosial Nights with de Quincey and Hogg (the Ettric Shepherd), etc., appear to have been distinctly ' wet ', and the visitors when they were hard up did not seem to hesitate to pocket the silver spoons and forks. When Professor Wilson died, the family had to hunt round all the pawn-shops in Edinburgh to recover the family plate. Coggie Ferrier, Mrs Rhodes' sister, usually lived with us, and her brother Walter was often a visitor, both of them great friends of Robert Louis Stevenson, and the recipients of many of his published letters ; but I never remember hearing anything of him at the time.

Hodson, a philosopher, writing a book on Ethics, was our nearest neighbour, and we often went long walks with him. He was a nephew of de Quincey, and I remember asking him if his uncle ever gave him opium, and he said, " Yes," when he was once unwell his uncle dosed him with opium as a remedy. I recall a visit from Lord Aberdare, the Home Secretary, whom I afterwards knew as President of the R.G.S., when first I read a paper to the Society. And one day three of us went over to Freshwater and paid a visit to Mrs Cameron, who shewed us all her wonderful photographic portraits.

From Bonchurch I went in October, 1868, to Trinity Hall, Cambridge, and lived at " Greefs ", 4, Kings Parade, where my brother Walter had lodged before me. Of my University career there is really not much to record, except to say that I had a delightful time, belonged to the Athenæum, the Pitt, and the A.D.C., where I used to play women's parts, and was a good deal at Newmarket. Times were good, money fairly plentiful, and champagne flowed freely. I won the Freshman's Hurdle Race, but the following winter, my brother having given me a mount for a day's hunting in the Vale of Aylesbury, on a very windy day, a gate broke away and gave me a compound fractured leg, and I was taken back to London and laid up in my brother's house for five or six weeks. When I was well enough, I went with him on a trip in his cutter yacht the *Volante* to Ireland, racing at Belfast and elsewhere. My mother usually took a house at Cowes or Ryde in the summer, and I had a good deal of yacht racing before and later. I was plucked for my "Little Go" the first time, but got through the second time, chiefly owing to my friend, Walter Durnford,[1] who had just become a fellow of King's, and used to insist on my going over to his rooms, where he stuffed me with Greek grammar. I failed once in the additional subjects, but got through the second time, and was then free to go my own way. I chose the Natural Science Tripos, and took Botany and Comparative Anatomy as special subjects. The student of the present day would smile at the Botanical instruction in those times. Professor Babington's lectures were dreadfully dull, and I made arrangements with Mr Mud, the head of the Botanical Gardens, to take me in hand. He was an illiterate Scotchman who smoked very strong tobacco and smelt strongly of whisky, but he knew his classification and grounded me in "Natural orders", and he used to supply me with specimens to dissect and describe. We would wander round the garden for an hour examining plants and talking botany, but if I ventured to say, "But, Mr Mud, Darwin says so and so", he used to dig his walking stick in the ground and turn round and glare at me and say, "Mr Mudsley" (as he called me), "that

---

[1] Sir Walter Durnford, later the Provost of King's College.

19

man Darwin will go to Hell ". I was luckier in my other studies, for I had already made friends with J. W. Clark, who was then Curator of the Museum of Comparative Anatomy, and gave me the run of the museum and helped me in every way. It was a friendship which lasted for his lifetime, and Scroope House, both in his mother's time and his wife's, was a second home to me. I worked with several " coaches ", principally with Marlborough Pryor and Francis Darwin, and eventually got a second class in the Tripos.

I had another friend in Alfred Newton, Professor of Zoology, and used on Sunday night to go to his rooms, where one met many interesting people.

I cannot leave my Cambridge friends without mentioning dear old Ben Latham, the Tutor of Trinity Hall. Ben, as he was always called, although his name was Henry, was a wonderful judge of character, and he knew exactly when a tight rein was necessary, and when a youth could be left to go his own way ; and he always had an amusing way of expressing his preferences. I tackled him once about a man whom he advised to leave the Hall or migrate to another college, saying I really did not think him a bad sort. " No ", said Ben, " but he had too many coats ". There was a friend of mine who, Ben said, was too effeminate, and when I stood up for him, saying he certainly did not row or play games, but that he was fond of riding, Ben replied, " No, he never rides " (he always slurred his r's), " he only goes for a promenade *à cheval*, and I believe he has frills to his nightshirt ". His judgment was right in both cases.

We had to go as undergraduates, for any breaches of discipline, cutting chapels, etc., to Hopkins, the Dean. He was the shyest of men, and when he had to blow one up, he always stood by the fireplace and looked at one in the looking glass, and every peccant undergraduate tried to manoeuvre so as to look him straight in the face, when the admonition would always fizzle out. I got to know him well later on, and liked him. There was much mystery at one time over the frequent visits of a Turk to Hoppy's rooms. It turned out that he had made up his mind to go to Khiva in the long vacation and was learning Turki, although he kept the matter dark.

I asked him later how he managed to get across the country which the Russians were so carefully guarding. He said it was quite easy, Russian Officers were always passing to the front, and when he met one at one of the Inns he would go up to him, if possible after dinner, and say, " I hear, Sir, you are going on to the front. I am going on myself to-morrow, and have a carriage and horses all ready to start, and as it is very dull travelling alone, it would give me great pleasure if you would take the vacant seat ". He told me they invariably jumped at the offer, so as to avoid the considerable expense. He always travelled in parsonical attire, black coat, white tie, and tall hat. Once the hat fell off while he was asleep, and he had to return many miles to retrieve it.

He got within a few days of Khiva when Skobeleff, who was in command, heard of him, and sent for him to his headquarters, and asked Hoppy what the mischief he was there for, and gave him a pretty good dressing down. Hoppy said he quite lost his temper with the general and told him what he thought of him, to which the general replied that he should go no further, and he would send him back with an escort at once. Hoppy said his temper was all right the next day, so he went to the general to say good-bye and said he hoped they would meet again, as he would come from India next time. However, his health prevented him ever trying to get to Khiva again.

Another of Hoppy's long vacation trips took him to Mexico, and he landed at Vera Cruz and took the coach to go to the City. In those days the coach was the only means of transport. At dawn the next morning, when approaching the City of Jalapa, the coach was set upon by brigands, who robbed poor Hoppy of everything, leaving him nothing but a shirt as covering. As he put it, " It was most awkward dodging about behind cactus hedges with nothing on but a shirt, and when I saw a man riding out of the City on what was evidently an English saddle, I thought he must be an Englishman, so I went up to him and said, ' I beg your pardon ! you might not know it, but I am a clergyman of the Church of England, and I do hope you can lend me a pair of trousers ' ".

I may add here that many years after, when I

was in Mexico, I learnt that it was the usual precautions in the coaching days when one had friends coming up from the port, to place newspapers and safety-pins under the seats, so that if brigands stripped the travellers they might have wherewith all to be clothed.

After I had taken my degree I registered on 29th January as a medical student, and attended lectures of Michael Foster and Sir George Humphrey, with both of whom I made friends, and I began human dissection.

The authorities of Trinity Hall asked me to become a " Fellow Commoner ", so as to join their Society at the High Table.

CHAPTER III

WEST INDIES AND AMERICA

My great desire now was to see a tropical forest, so in June, 1872, I persuaded my brother Charles to come with me to the West Indies, and we sailed on the 17th in the R.M.S. *Tagus*, Captain Woolward, and touched at Barbados, St Thomas, and Jackmel, reaching Jamaica on the 31st. We travelled about for a fortnight, finding people most hospitable. We met Captain Lanyon, then a Captain in a West Indian Regiment (later on Sir Owen Lanyon of South African fame), the Governor's A.D.C., who brought us an invitation from Sir John Peter Grant to stay with him at Craigton, his house in the mountains. There we stayed until the 21st July, when we sailed in R.M.S. *Nile*, Captain Revett, for Colon.

We crossed the isthmus of Panama in the railway, and I was amused to find that tickets were freely given to anyone going across for a trip and back to Colon, but £5 was charged for a ticket for all passengers who had to cross and were not returning at once. It took four hours doing the forty-five miles ; the first twenty miles were mostly swamp, and then came some fine tropical forest.

The Grand Hotel at Panama, where we stayed,

seemed to be the centre of Panama civilization. There was a roulette table in the hall every afternoon and evening, and the queerest mixture of nationalities and colours, who swarmed round and planked down their dollars very freely. We met Captain Mannering, whom we had known in England, of H.M.S. gunboat *Chameleon*, which was lying some miles off shore, and made acquaintance with some of the officers of the American man-of-war *California*. On Sunday afternoon we went with all the *élite* to the cockpits. Cock-fighting seemed to be the chief interest in Panama, and there was the greatest excitement over the battles, and lots of money changed hands.

One day Captain Mannering asked us to go with him to pay his official visit to the *California*. It was a long hot row in Mannering's gig to the American ship. We were piped up on board, and shewn into the Captain's cabin, but the cabin was empty. Presently a face covered with soap-lather was thrust between the curtains at the end of the cabin and a voice said, " Gentlemen, I am very glad to see you. What will you drink ? If you take our champagne, take some bitters with it ; it's too sweet ", then the head disappeared as rapidly as it had appeared. A few minutes later, Captain Clitz came in, shaved and in uniform ; the formal introductions were made, and we drank champagne and bitters. Then the Captain rang the bell and said to the orderly, " Ask the Chief executive officer to step this way ". The Chief executive officer appeared ; more formal introductions, and we had to drink champagne and bitters with him. The same proceeding took place with each of the ward-room officers. Then the band played, and we were shewn round the ship. To every gun there was a fighting cock tied by the leg. These were victors of the previous Sunday's battles, bought by the officers, fed up and taken back to fight the following Sunday.

After this we went to the ward-room, and the ward-room produced sherry, and we were introduced, with drinks, to each of the gun-room officers.

When we were leaving, Captain Mannering said, " Captain Clitz, I had always heard that the American Navy was so strict about the prohibition of spirituous liquor on board its ships ".

" Yes, Captain Mannering ", said Clitz, " that is quite true, but you see our doctor is so kind about medical comforts."

We had the long row back in the afternoon heat. About halfway in we met a shore-boat rowed by two negroes, and a man stood up in the stern and shouted to us. " Lay on your oars ", said Mannering, " and let us see what he wants. " It proved to be an American Officer whose acquaintance we had made at the hotel. When he came within speaking distance he shouted, " Been to see Old Clitz ? " " Yes ", we yelled. " Full of rum ? " was the reply, which was too much for the gravity of our bluejackets.

On the 29th July we sailed in the ss. *Guatemala*, Captain Douglas, for San José de Guatemala and reached that port on 6th August. We were in sight of land and the long range of volcanoes most of the way, and the volcano of Managua was smoking. We called at several small ports, and encountered a terrific thunderstorm in the Gulf of Nicoya. We were unable to land cargo at La Union in the beautiful Gulf of Fonseca, as the usual revolution was going on, and the town was holding a fiesta and firing rockets in honour of a victory. Not long before our arrival the Republic of Honduras had indulged in a navy, consisting of one armed schooner. One of the steamers of the line in which we were travelling came into port, and the Captain landed to do some business in the town, and on returning to the steamer in his boat was astonished at a shot being fired across his bow. "Row on", he said, "it is clearly some mistake"; but a second shot came closer, and it was evident they were trying to hit him. This was too much for the fat and irascible skipper; he reached his steamer (which was already under weigh) in a towering rage, shouted to his mate to "clear for action", and proceeded to engage the Hondurarian navy with his signal gun. This was luckily of fair size, and his mate happened to be an old naval gunner. The projectiles were any bits of old iron they could find, but, keeping his steamer on the move to avoid the shots from the schooner, which was at anchor, he managed to leave her a comparative wreck, and then steamed away with the stars and stripes flying.

It turned out that the Captain had broken some new rule that no boat should leave without permission from the Captain of the Port. There was no end of protest and diplomatic correspondence, but finally the peace of the world was ensured.

San José de Guatemala is even now a miserable place ; in those days it consisted of the custom-house and a few shanties. We had great difficulty in engaging mules to take us inland, and we did not get off until noon the next day. After leaving the swamp the track led through the dense forest, and my chief remembrance is of the marvellous profusion of butterflies of all sizes and colouring, showing like a tesselated pavement on the damp patches in the track, and rising like a bouquet of bright flowers on our approach.

As we started so late on such wretched animals, and had forty-four miles to ride to Esquintla, of course we were benighted, and did not reach our destination until ten o'clock. I well remember the last part of the ride. We were in a strange country about which we had been told hair-raising tales of the dangers of travelling ; we could not speak or understand the language, and it was a very dark night.

Our half-caste guide rode a white horse, and I could just manage to keep a white blur in front of me ; so I kept a loaded revolver handy in my pocket in case of accidents. Of course it was quite safe, and the wild stories one had heard at Panama were mostly inventions. From Esquintla we travelled in the diligence to the capital, where we put up at the Globe Hotel.

My friend, Osbert Salvin, who had passed some years collecting birds and studying the natural history of Guatemala, had given me letters to Mr Nelson, a coffee planter, and he and his agent, Mr Whitney, were most helpful in making arrangements for our trip through the Altos. We had arrived at the time of the great Jocotenango fair, which gave us a chance of seeing the city at its best, and the Indians who crowded into the city in their native costume. We were hospitably entertained by Mr Corbet, the English Chargé d'Affaires, Mr Magee and others, but the dinner I remember best was given us about three o'clock in the afternoon by a Guatemalteco fellow passenger at a little restaurant kept by a Frenchman, who spoke delightfully broken English, and cooked and served the dinner himself. It was a most excellent dinner, and as we had had nothing decent to eat for many days we did justice to it. When I thought it was all over, imagine my horror when the Frenchman came into the room carrying a huge plum pudding on fire! "This", he cried, beaming with pride, "is what the Englishman always eats", and he proceeded to pile up my plate with it. This, after a good dinner, with the thermometer over 80°! But I struggled on manfully, and then followed the inevitable bottle of sweet champagne.

After a week in the city we started on a trip for a fortnight through the Altos, Antigua, and Quetzaltenango, down to the Costa Grande to Las Nubes, Mr Nelson's coffee finca, and back by the Lake of

Atitlan. It was a very enjoyable trip, but this country is described in *A Glimpse at Guatemala,* [1] and I need say no more about it here. After a few days in Guatemala City we rode to the port, and on the way met Mr Sarg, [2] and stayed with him for the day or two we had to remain at San José. Thus commenced a friendship which endured until his death in 1920.

On the 9th September we sailed in the ss. *San Salvador* for Acapulco, touching at several small ports on the way ; and four days later we left in ss. *Constitution* for San Francisco, which we reached on the 27th September. When landing at Acapulco, or some of the other ports on the coast, Charlie had contracted a malarious fever, which was very severe for some time.

After a few days in San Francisco we left for the big trees and the Yosemite Valley. The railway then went only as far as Merced, and next morning we were to take the coach. The landlord said to me, " Well, I guess you boys will have a good time, as there is a party of ladies from the East going with you ". To which I replied, " Then I think we will wait for the coach next day ". But he replied, " Then you won't see the Yosemite, for this is the last coach going towards the valley this year ". So I met my fate ! for the party consisted of Mrs Morris and her two daughters, [3] and a Mrs Cass and her

[1] A glimpse at Guatemala by A. C. and A. P. Maudslay. John Murray, 1899.

[2] Afterwards Imperial German Consul.

[3] Some years later Miss Morris became my wife.

daughter, who had come across the continent with a party of railway directors, who had left San Francisco for the North to locate the future terminus of the Northern Pacific Railway. The rest of the way to the Yosemite was done on mule-back.

When we returned to San Francisco we found great excitement over the reported discovery of a diamond mine. It appears that a Greaser, that is, a Mexican, had gone into the Bank of California carrying an old sardine tin containing some stones, which he turned out on the counter and asked if they were of any value. They proved to be diamonds, and the man said he knew there were more like them at a spot he knew in Arizona. Of course an expedition was at once despatched, and its leader sent back to say they had reached the spot and found some more diamonds. This was enough to start a rush, and the town was bubbling with excitement. We dined one night with Dr Blake, a man of science, and I asked him what he thought of the reports. He told me he thought it was a fraud, but could give me no reason except that he had asked if there were any termite hills where the diamonds were found, and was told there were none, and he said he had never heard of diamonds being found in a country where there were no white ant-nests. It was an odd reason to give, but he was right about the fraud. For on my return later to Cambridge I was dining one night with Campbell of Trinity Hall, who had rowed in the University Boat Race the year before, and had then disappeared ;

31

and he told me that he had gone out to South Africa, where his brother was conducting a gold convoy from the mines, or some such rather risky work, and that his sister-in-law was left alone in some out-of-the-way place, and he had been appealed to go and look after her—that he had found things all right and there was no need for him to stay, so he had gone to the diamond mines and worked there until he had made enough money for a few months' hunting trip, and had then returned to Cambridge to finish his course and take his degree.

When I told him about the Arizona find he said, "Oh, we know all about that, and actually know some of the diamonds that were shown at the Bank. It was all arranged by some Jew buyers in South Africa, who had the ground salted in Arizona, and when the news of the supposed discovery reached South Africa, down went the price of diamonds and the plotters scooped the market".

After a trip with the Morrises to the Geysers, which were not interesting, we left for Salt Lake City, where we spent two days, and called on Brigham Young, but unluckily he had just gone out of town. Here we were overtaken by the Morrises and the railroad party, who kindly took us as far as Niagara in their private car. Herds of buffalo and antelope could be seen from the train, and the ground was often strewn with buffalo bones. A great district in Chicago was still derelict from the devastation caused by the great fire. At Niagara we found all the cab-horses going about with blankets over them and mufflers round their necks, just recovering from an epidemic known as epizootic. And as the horses had to be taken out for gentle exercise and the tourist season was over, we were followed about by strings of cabs bidding for a fare.

From Niagara we went to New York, where we found the Brasseys in the *Eothen*, and spent one day with them going over the Government establishments on the Islands, Sing Sing Lunatic Asylum, etc. We were in the city during election day, and witnessed the excitement when the returns came in and General Grant was elected President. We met Nick Kane and Tom Newbolt and some other old Cambridge friends, and were entertained by them, and went on some expeditions with the Morrises; then, hearing of the great fire at Boston, we started off there as soon as our engagements allowed. The fire was over, but still smouldering, and as the sparks beat against the face of our hotel, a fireman, to whom I spoke, suggested that it would be wise to go to bed in my boots. Next day we watched the fire engines at work, and people digging out their iron safes from the ruins. All the streets were guarded by soldiers.

After this we went to Cambridge and were shewn over Harvard; dined with Professor Goodwin and met pleasant people. Then we returned to New York, said good-bye to the Morrises, and sailed in the Cunard ss. *Cuba* for Liverpool on 27th November, landing at Liverpool on 8th December.

On the 11th I went back to Cambridge. My

younger brother, Eustace, had come up to Trinity Hall, and we lived together at Greefs. I went on with my work until June, 1873, when Eustace and I started on a trip to Iceland. I had gained a little experience of mule travel in Central America, and saw to it that our equipment included good pack-saddles with boxes to fit them, and sufficient spare girths, halters, etc.

CHAPTER IV

ICELAND

We left Granton on 1st June, 1873, in the Danish ss. *Diana*, an old gunboat changed into a mail steamer. There were thirty-eight passengers on board, which was more than she had ever carried before, and we slept round the main cabin, and accommodation was primitive.

What was our disgust on arriving at Thorshaven in the Faroe Islands to find that half our baggage had been left behind, although we had taken every precaution and had been assured by the agent that it was all safely stored in the hold. We entrusted letters and telegrams to fishing boats and others in hope that some of them would reach the agent. On leaving Thorshaven we passed through the narrow strait between the two islands and had a fine view of the magnificent cliff. As soon as we were through the passage the entrance was lost to sight, and the huge semicircle of black cliffs (some of them 2,000 feet high) seemed to hang over us, with the great waves of a grey sea breaking into white foam on the base, and vivid patches of green grass contrasting with a grey sky. It was a wonderfully impressive sight.

35

We reached Reykjavik on the 8th June, and made arrangements with Gier Zuga, whom we had heard of as a guide, for the hire of ponies for a trip to Thingvalla and the Geysers, until the rest of our baggage arrived and we could buy enough ponies for our proposed trip round the Island.

As I knew the Njala Saga (the story of Burnt Njal) well and the story of Gretter the Strong, I was much interested in Thingvalla and its neighbourhood. We camped at the Geyser and kept watch for two days; we saw two eruptions of the Great Geyser, and baited Strokr with turf and made it erupt many times. I have since seen the Geysers of New Zealand and of the Yellowstone; and though not so large as some of the Yellowstone Geysers the Great Geyser of Iceland is as perfect as any, and resembles Old Faithful in the Yellowstone, but does not erupt nearly so often.

On our return to Reykjavik we found our missing luggage had arrived, and after a few days of preparation we started on our long journey on 24th June, having secured Thorgrimer Gudmanson as interpreter, and Gizli as ponyman. Thorgrimer's English was very sketchy, as it had been learnt principally from some Scotch horse-dealers; but it improved rapidly, and he turned out a first-rate fellow, and has, I believe, since become the chief Icelandic guide. We started with sixteen ponies, and bought two or three others during our journey—two riding ponies for each of us, and two for each pack. The pack-saddles answered well, and I was very glad we had brought

36

a good supply of halters, as the common Icelandic practice was to tie a rope round the pony's lower jaw, and we frequently found the pony's tongue badly cut, sometimes almost cut in half.

We had intended climbing Hekla and then getting inland to the Fiskavatn, a series of little-known lakes, but owing to the very bad weather and the flooding of the rivers both enterprizes had to be given up.

The most difficult part of the journey was in passing round the great mass of the Vatna Jokul, where the glaciers came close to the sea, and the streams that flowed from them are nearly as broad as they are long. Our stopping places were isolated farms, where we could find a little rough pasturage for our ponies. The houses were usually holes in the hillsides, faced with wood. Such roofs as projected were thickly covered with turf.

The following extracts from a rough diary give some idea of the conditions of travel :—

29th June.—Storivellir to Breithbolstadr.

The minister wished to stop us, but we thought it best to push on. Such storms of wind and rain for the first hour, then sent Gizli to hunt for a farmer to guide us across the river. The guide led one pony across while we drove in the others, but they all turned down-stream into deep water, and we had the pleasure of seeing the ponies swimming about with all our packs under water. When they got to the other side, the bank was so high where they touched that they could not climb up it. So they all turned round again and swam back to the place they started from. Of course we had to follow and drive them across again, having to cross the river in all three times. The water was halfway up our saddle-flaps. After an hour's ride over a most dismal sandy plain in the pelting rain we came to another river. It looked shallow, and with the help of the local guide we started to cross it, and again the pack-ponies got into deep water and all our boxes and bedding were swamped. We spent the following day trying to dry our clothes.

The next day we rode from Breithabolsted to Skoger, crossing numerous streams running over the sandy plain between the mountains and the sea, the ponies frequently getting into quicksand, but gamely struggling out again. At Skoger we came to a halt, as Eustace was suffering tortures from toothache, and his face was dreadfully swollen with the formation of an abcess. The only instrument we had with us was the pincers used for drawing nails from the pony's shoes, and these were too big to get into Eustace's mouth. We were at our wits' end, when we heard that a doctor lived some distance away, but that he had gone for a week to Reykjavik. However, hoping that he might have left some instruments behind him, I sent a man off with three ponies to beg the loan of instruments from the doctor's wife. My messenger did the journey in record time, and returned the following afternoon with a bundle of instruments, luckily including a

38

good pair of forceps. However, the face was too much swollen for one to do anything that day, but the day following I was able to pull the tooth out, and Eustace said I gave him very little pain ; the relief was immediate, but he was not fit to travel until the 6th July, when we went to Vik. We stayed at Vik for three days, as Eustace's face was still discharging and giving him a good deal of pain. The real danger in crossing the rivers which flowed from the glaciers over the sandy plain was on account of the quicksands. Our procedure was for the guide to go first with one led pony, then for the four of us to follow in line, each leading three or four ponies each tied head to tail, and this is where our halters proved so useful. The leader would often flounder into quicksand, but if he managed to get across, the sand would get harder as each pony struggled through it. Often the leader had to turn back, as he began to sink too deep. The ponies were wonderful, they never gave up, but always worked their legs as hard as they could, and the sand grew firmer under them. However, it is anything but a pleasant sensation to feel one's pony sinking under one.

We had three days' similar travel, crossing streams all the time. On the 13th we reached the farm of Nupstathr, from which we hoped to get into the mountains and see, and if possible, secure one of the wild sheep in what is known as the Nupstathr Skoger or forest. The farmer did not seem to like us going to the forest, and said the rivers were not

fordable, etc., but as his information was rather
vague we decided to go and see for ourselves. We
took Gudmanson and three pack-ponies with food
and tent and secured a youth for guide. It was a
beautiful afternoon. After going a short distance
round a bold headland, the boy said that we could
go no farther without crossing the Nupstathr river,
and that would be impossible; however, he would
try for a ford. At last he returned with the joyful
news that he had found a ford, so off we started.
The river was very deep, but not so bad as I expected,
and none of the packs got wet. Gudmanson once
went deep into a quicksand, but his pony struggled
out gamely.

The wind was coming straight down the valley,
raising the sands in clouds a hundred feet high, and
it was awful work making head against it. For
about three quarters of an hour we toiled across
the sand, picking our way carefully over the rough
ground between the numerous sand-pits, most of
them filled with water. It is difficult to give an
idea what this part of the sand was like. Perhaps
more than anything like a very rough beach above
high water-mark, full of pits from two to twelve
feet deep. Sometimes our ponies stepped into small
sand-holes, and it was hard work in the blinding sand
to keep them out of the large ones. In front, to the
right, I could see what appeared to be a large lava
field, very black looking. At last we came to a
glacier stream which poured its water into the river
we had crossed. This was the Sula, and our guide

pronounced it unfordable. Gudmanson was game
to try it, but it looked too bad, and we would not
let him. The guide then said we could go no farther,
but it looked so short a distance over the glacier
to the hills beyond that I hoped there might be
some way of getting on to them. The guide offered
to go with me on foot to see how far the ponies
could go without actually getting on to the ice;
but said he thought it very dangerous to take them
any farther. So Eustace stayed with the ponies
while Gudmanson and I went with the guide. We
picked our way between the pits for a short time
and were near the side of a small glacier stream,
when our guide, who was going first, suddenly disappeared through the crust of the sand. Gudmanson
was close behind him, and I caught hold of his coat
and we rolled together down the slope towards the
stream. As soon as we recovered ourselves we
clambered on hands and knees up to the hole and
could see the guide about five feet below the surface
struggling with the sand that had fallen in on him;
with Gudmanson's long arms and the help of my
leather belt we managed to pull him out, but he
was a good deal shaken and bruised about the head,
so we returned to the ponies and looked out for a
spot to camp. We found a level space near the
riverside and pitched our tent. It was luckily a
beautiful night, and the wind had fallen, so the
guide returned to Nupstathr with the ponies, with
instructions to come as early as possible in the morning
and bring some milk and our Alpine rope.

14th July.—We slept very soundly, but no guide appeared, and we had plenty of time to look about us. Huge blocks of ice were sticking up through the sand all around us, and about two hundred yards off the glacier was quite clear. All the ice was jet black from the volcanic sand frozen into it.

We were debating whether to try and get to the Skoger without a guide with the help of the tent ropes, when two men appeared, sent from the farm to guide us, as our guide from the day before was too bad to come. It was now twelve o'clock, and they said they had started at five and had been all this time finding a ford, which I hardly believed. They brought bread, milk and our rope, and we gave them food and whisky. Then, roped together, we started for the glacier. It was easy walking once we were on the ice, and it took us only half an hour to get across it, then we had less than an hour's walk on the sand and then half an hour's very rough scramble along the side of the hill bordering the river, which here had a lake-like expansion. There was a little wood on the hillside, then we came to more level ground where the wood was thicker. While at lunch, we saw some of the wild sheep on the hills, and from the way they skipped over the rocks I thought that it would need a deal of stalking to get near them. After lunch we walked through the wood (which was here fairly thick, and in places about seven feet high), and tried to get a sight of the waterfall. We did not succeed very well, as the rocks shut out the view of the fall itself; but the surrounding scenery was very picturesque. We returned to the tent and slept there, and the guides returned to Nupstathr.

15th July.—The guides came back about nine o'clock and we packed and washed up, not an easy thing to do with the water at 30°. Met Gizli and the ponies. The first part of the way was over small glacier streams, some of them with bad quicksands —so bad that they could not bear the weight of us on our ponies, so we had to lead them. The sand was still broken up by pits, but after an hour or so we came to firmer ground, although it was a rough road all day and we were continually crossing glacier streams. About half-past four we came to the Skuthara river. All day we had been passing the Skuthara Yokull, an enormous glacier of black ice, fifteen or more miles across, and this was its principal stream; for over an hour and a half we were fording its numerous branches, which were very swift and deep, and full of quicksands. We were a cavalcade of twenty-five ponies to-day, eighteen of ours, one of the guide's, and six of the Knapavellir farmers. The guides divided the ponies as equally as possible, Eustace and I each leading two. Once the guide went in over the pony's back; only the pony's head and neck and the top of the saddle was visible above the sand; but the man rolled off, and we managed somehow to pull the pony out and also the one he was leading, the others breaking away and getting back to a sandbank. The ponies struggle very gamely and never give

43

in. At last we got through the last stream, and went on to Sandfete, where we slept in the church, a small wooden box-like building. Luckily it was a still day, so we were not troubled with sand-storms.

I had secured from the farmer at Nupstathr two heads of the wild sheep, which are now in the museum at Cambridge.

Two more days' ride over similar country brought us to the end of this range of mountains; at one spot there was not more than half a mile between the glacier and the sea.

The scenery now changed completely; for we left snow mountains and glaciers for fiords and terraced trap-hills, reaching Eskiford on the 26th July, where we visited the Iceland spar-mines, and bought some specimens; one is now in the Cambridge Museum.

We now travelled through much more liveable country; the farms were better and some of the scenery very fine. On the 4th August we left Grimstader to visit the waterfall of Detifoss. It was a gray morning, with storms of wind and rain as we rode over the rather desolate country through great broken masses of black lava, and now and then over what looked like a pavement formed of the tops of basaltic columns. However, it cleared up as we approached the fall, which is V-shaped and of no great size, but curiously and weirdly picturesque. The chasm is surrounded by broken blocks and cliffs of black basalt, and as the spray blows aside, one sees the water breaking on the tops of detached basalt pillars of varying heights, and this gives a great appearance of depth to the chasm; the colouring too is most curious, black rocks, a gray sky, gray glacier water breaking into white foam and spray, and patches of vivid green moss and grass wherever it gets a foothold.

A few days later, on the 11th August, we met William Morris and his friend, Mr Faulkner, who had just come across the Springisandr; we went back to the farm and had coffee together, and then parted as they were going in the opposite direction.

Arriving at Sjosavatn, we went to see the fall of Godifoss. It had none of the weird charm of Detifoss, the water beautifully clear and the surroundings picturesque; and in shape it was like a miniature Niagara. On the 12th August we reached Akureyri, the second port in Iceland. Here we met two young Americans, Sam Howland and W. Bechman, and travelled in company for the next few days. On the 19th I see my diary comes to an abrupt end, but we continued our journey round the north of the island usually in pleasant weather.

On our way from Reykjavik we had noticed a farm on the River Sog, issuing from the Lake of Thingvallir, where the pasture was above the very poor average, and where the river looked fishable. So there we went at the end of our journey, and stayed at the farm to rest and fatten our ponies before selling them at Reykjavik. The fishing proved first-rate: in five days we caught three hundred-weight of trout and char, the biggest scaling just over ten pounds Out of one pool I took eighty pounds weight of fish with an artificial bait; the water was deep, clear and very swift, and the bank at this pool too steep and high for using a fly, but in other parts there was capital fly water. Our trouble was not with artificial but natural flies. They rose in swarms such as I have never seen before or since; they did not bite or sting, but crawled over one and tickled horribly. We wore our water-proofs, and sou'-westers with veils sewn into them and the veils tucked into our coats; and even with these precautions the flies managed to crawl inside. While I was fishing my lucky pool, my brother was fishing down-stream, and after a time I lost sight of him and learnt from Thorgrimer that he was on the hill, so I sent him up a three-pounder to show him what I was doing. This brought no response, so I sent him up a seven-pounder; this brought a shout, but he did not appear, so I climbed up the bank and hillside to see what was the matter, and there I found him sitting on a hill-top trying to catch the breeze, just like a picture I remember in Punch of Mr Briggs in the Highlands with a crowd of flies around him. The irritation had been so great that Eustace had thrown down his rod and made a bolt for it, and as he had no remembrance of where he had thrown his rod, it took us nearly an hour to find it. However, we moved down the river where the flies were not so bad, and the fish still rose gaily.

We took a pannier pony one morning to carry the

fish. He was a bright piebald before we came to a damp, rather steep dip in the moor, and when he came up the other side, you could not tell the colour through the thick coating of crawling flies. This sounds like a traveller's tale, but it is no exaggeration. Thank goodness, when there was a strong breeze and in open ground we were not much troubled with the pest, but we always wore veils.

Our ponies picked up wonderfully with a few days' rest, and the farmer absolutely refused to accept any payment, saying we had more than paid him with the fish, which he had salted down for the winter.

At Reykjavik we met Morris and his friend and the two Americans. We danced at Mrs Magnussen's sister's wedding, with ladies wearing fourteenth-century head-dresses. We foreigners were all invited to a banquet in our honour, at which old Dr Hjaltalin was in the chair, the same who had presided at the celebrated banquet described by Lord Dufferin in *Letters from High Latitudes*. But none of us made a Latin speech when our healths were drunk, and all our efforts failed to persuade Morris to reply in Icelandic.

We made a very good sale of our eighteen ponies and were congratulated by Icelanders on their condition after such a long journey, which was greatly due to the efficient pack-saddles and halters.

All six of us foreigners returned home on the *Diana*—a fine passage and a cheerful one, for Morris's stories never failed. He was not at all

47

the professional raconteur, for his stories, often racy ones, bubbled over as though he could not help it. At last the Captain said he would put him in irons if he kept him up another night, as he had been given no sleep. Certainly Morris was not what one might have pictured to oneself as the author of *The Earthly Paradise*. I am sorry I never met him again, and only saw him once, many years later, thumping a tub in Hyde Park. He was exploited by the Socialists. I was told that his daughter married a plumber, and that he said he " Didn't mind that, but the damned fellow couldn't plumb ".

CHAPTER V

TRINIDAD AND AUSTRALIA

In October I returned to Cambridge, but I was always so much troubled with coughs and catarrh that I gave up all idea of medical study, and fled to the tropics. In January, 1874, I sailed for the West Indies in a Royal Mail steamer with the intention of growing tobacco in Jamaica, as there were a number of refugees from Havana in Jamaica at that time who understood the cultivation of tobacco and were seeking employment. However, among my fellow passengers were Neville Lubbock [1] the head of the Colonial Company, and Tom Hill of the Colonial Bank, and as we found that there was a strict quarantine in Jamaica, which would have entailed an unpleasant delay, they persuaded me to go on with them to Trinidad.

First of all I put up at the only hotel at Port of Spain, and never have I passed such a night! I woke up after half an hour's sleep and killed six or eight bugs on my bed with the end of the match with which I had lighted the candle; the whole place was swarming with them. In the morning I pulled up some of the half-rotten wall-paper which was

[1] Afterwards Sir Neville Lubbock, K.C.M.G., President of the West Indian Association.

49

hanging on the wall, and found a black mass of bugs underneath. Luckily I was delivered from this by the kindness of Mr J. Bell Smyth, who took me to his charming house on the Savannah. When inviting me he said, "You won't mind me asking you to examine your luggage very carefully before bringing it into the house, for I have heard of the reputation of that hotel". Luckily, I did not bring any other visitors with me. The Smyths were kindness itself. They had a nice red-headed boy I used to play with, and some years ago when at a Military Tournament I saw a red-headed Captain Bell Smyth presented with a shield as a prize as the champion man-at-arms in the British Army, and I feel sure he was my little playfellow. Mrs Smyth was partly French, and they were Roman Catholics; I remember being solemnly blessed by a Bishop for decorating the oratory for a festival with the gorgeous tropical flowers that grew around the house in such profusion. Then I went to stay with Lubbock at the Colonial Company's Estate of Petit Marne, where he had set up the first Usine Central in the British West Indies. Lubbock had worked hard at Sugar Manufacture in all its branches, in France, England and the West Indies, so all his newly installed machinery was up-to-date, and I spent some time with him in his laboratory being initiated into the mysteries of sugar chemistry.

I returned with Lubbock to the Smyth's, dined at Government House, and made the acquaintance of Mr Longden, who was just finishing his term as

Governor. Then Lubbock asked me to go with him to Barbados, where he was interested in some sugar refineries; and Mr and Mrs Longden were among our fellow passengers. After a week or so in Barbados we sailed again for Trinidad, where I had some idea of starting as a cacao planter. Among our fellow-passengers was Mr William Cairns, who had just finished his term as governor of British Honduras, and had been appointed to succeed Mr Longden at Trinidad. Mr Cairns was half-brother to Lord Cairns, the Lord Chancellor, and had passed much of his life as a Civil Servant in Ceylon. The second day of our voyage together he asked me if I would become his Private Secretary, saying that the appointment might be only temporary, as he was expecting someone out from England. Thinking it would be an interesting experience, I accepted, and much to the amusement of my Trinidad friends I stepped ashore as His Excellency's Private Secretary.

Government House had been burnt down some years before, and was now in the process of being rebuilt, the Governors having for some time lived in what was known as the Cottage in the Botanical Garden. It was at the Cottage that Charles Kingsley, when the guest of Sir Arthur Gordon, had written *At Last*. It was quite a comfortable house for the Tropics, and had a good swimming bath. We took over some of the old servants, and as there was no A.D.C., all the household management fell to my share. I had a vegetable garden, and two coolies of the convict gang to cultivate it. One was a

Chinaman and the other a Hindoo, and they despised one another as gardeners : each one, when he got a chance, recited to me in pidgin English the list of the heinous crimes of which the other had been convicted, the Chinaman always ending with " He no good, he no savey Englishy Pea ".

I had the run of that beautiful Botanical Garden which has been tended as such for a hundred years. The Secretarial work was easy enough, but what was my surprise at the end of a few weeks to be told to send a telegram to Lord Carnarvon, the Secretary of State, for the Colonies, to the effect that the Governor was in bad health and asked for three months leave of absence. As Cairns had been for three years in British Honduras, leave was of course immediately granted, and he departed for England· in the next steamer, leaving me in charge of Government House and the servants.

I had bought a very nice pony and used to ride to my office in the town ; but as the acting Governor (who was Mr Bush the Colonial Secretary) had plenty of assistants in his office, he very seldom required my services, and I don't think I did anything more serious than issue invitations to a Queen's Birthday Ball. So I had a very easy time.

Trinidad Society is very pleasant, and the people most hospitable. I dined out and danced, went on fishing excursions to the Bocas, and spent some days shooting in the Highwoods. I passed a profitable time with Warner, an Inspector of Emigrants at San Fernando, who was visiting various estates and inquiring into the condition and treatment of the Indian coolies, and I was much surprised with the smoothness and equity with which the system worked.

The two front rows of seats in the San Fernando church were occupied by very voluminous darkie women, gorgeously arrayed and with the most amazing bonnets, and I learnt that they were all the wives of Chinamen; and thereby hangs a tale. At one time some of the planters became discontented with their Indian coolie workmen, and got the idea into their heads that Chinamen would suit them better; so pressure was brought to bear on the Government to send an agent to China to recruit Chinese labourers. The agent was specially instructed to recruit only in the agricultural districts, and he succeeded in engaging three hundred agricultural labourers. These he brought safely down to the port, only to find that there had been some delay in equipping the vessel he had chartered for the voyage; so he hired a large go-down wherein to camp the Chinamen during the few days' delay. Each Chinaman was furnished with a ticket of identification, and, a few at a time, they were allowed to go into the City to make purchases. When the vessel was ready, three hundred Chinamen all provided with identification tickets were safely got on board, but trouble started on the voyage; they proved to be a most unruly lot, and there was the greatest difficulty in enforcing order. When on arrival they were drafted off to the different plantations, matters grew worse, and there were more murders and serious crimes than had been known in the Island for years. Several Chinamen were hanged, and at last the truth leaked out.

Chinamen are very much alike to a European who has not lived long among them; and it appears that the simple agricultural labourers who had been allowed into the City had been hocussed and drugged by the scum of a Treaty Port, and their clothes and identification tickets had been taken from them. Thus the agent had succeeded in embarking some of the worst cut-throats in China, who were delighted at the chance of escaping from their country. However, they were Chinamen, and the survivors, finding that they were well and fairly treated, eventually settled down to work, and did well, marrying black wives, and proving good and indulgent husbands. Hence the gorgeous display in San Fernando church.

About six weeks after the Governor left I received a letter from him, telling me that he was not returning to Trinidad; so I was left in the lurch, and thought the best thing to do was to return home, where I arrived about July.

It had always been a great regret to me that I could not speak French, and as my brother Eustace was also wishing to learn French for an army examination, we agreed to go to France with the intention of living in a French family. We went to Tours and arrived just before dinner at the principal hotel; and as we entered the table d'hôte we were greeted by shouts of " Here is another " and found about twenty young Englishmen, many of whom we knew, who had all come on the same errand.

Next morning I called on a Frenchman to whom I had been recommended, who took pupils to live with his family, and found him full up. So we had to look for someone else. Meanwhile, we passed a week or two visiting the chateaux of the Loire, and I was just on the point of arranging to live with a curé at Blois, when I received a letter from Mr Cairns telling me that he had been appointed Governor of Queensland, and offering me the post of his Private Secretary, the salary being £400 a year and no expenses. So I wrote back accepting his offer.

I met Cairns in London, and did some shopping for our new home. Then he went to the Continent, and we met in November at Venice. I had never been in Venice before, and was determined to do the Grand Canal in a gondola; I did it wrapped up in an Ulster and all the rugs I could lay my hands on, for it was bitterly cold! We sailed in a P. & O. steamer to Alexandria and then went by train to Suez, where we met the P. & O. *Kaizer-i-Hind*, and changed steamers at Galle. I had always heard much of the P. & O. service, but unluckily met it when it was at the lowest point of its fortunes. The steamer in which we had passage from Galle was poorly found and most uncomfortable, and coal was piled up on deck to abaft the main mast, and the coal dust often blew over us. And she was so deeply laden that we could not open our portholes while going through the tropics. Captain MacCarthy,

Mr Cairns' A.D.C., had joined us at Venice, and I shared a cabin with him. He had recently returned from the Ashantee Campaign, and was still suffering occasionally from fever; and the rats, which were plentiful in our cabin, drove him wild; but when he took to trying to spit them with his sword I thought it time to make up a bed on a table outside.

Sir William Robinson and his wife were among our fellow passengers. He was on his way to govern Western Australia, and she, poor woman, was never free from sea-sickness during the whole of the voyage —a poor look-out for a colonial Governor's wife. We broke down for twenty-four hours about half way to Australia, but they patched the engines up again. At King George's Sound we went ashore and picked wildflowers. Here we left the Robinsons and took on board Sir Frederick Weld, who was leaving the Government of Western Australia for that of Tasmania. At Glenelg I left my Chief and went ashore to spend the day with some cousins, who had come down from Adelaide to meet me. Cairns, Weld and another official (I forget who it was) said they would go ashore unattended, as they expected to be met and taken up to Government House in Adelaide; but there was some muddle, and the three Excellencies were left to kick their heels about all day and lunch at a pot-house in the port. And as I returned to embark I found three disgruntled Excellencies walking back along the pier, with an A.D.C. in uniform marching after them and muttering apologies, to which little heed was paid. The comic paper in Adelaide did not forget to rub it in with a cartoon.

I found Sir Fred Weld charming, and he pressed me to come and pay him a visit in Tasmania when I could get a holiday.

At Melbourne we were fêted and taken to see the sights. One big dinner was given us by the Acting Governor, and I thought I was in for a dull evening, for my neighbour never opened his mouth except to eat during the first courses. Then he suddenly nudged me and said, "They look very grand, don't they, in their ribbons and orders?" and proceeded most interestingly to give me the history of all the notabilities present. When I asked him how he came to Melbourne he said, "Oh! I came as the Bank of New South Wales, and lived in a tent and slept on the cash-box, and then put up the first wooden shanty where the City of Melbourne now stands". We found in port H.M.S. *Barracouta*, Captain Stevens in command, with orders to take us to Brisbane. The *Barracouta* was an ancient paddle-ship, and our progress was slow.

Before we had got to the end of our long voyage from Venice I had begun to have doubts whether the position I held was a possible one. Mr Cairns, or Sir William Cairns as he had now become, was a very odd man. Many years of what I expect was a rather lonely life in Ceylon had not made him more sociable. He could be very pleasant at times, but his moods were fitful; and his digestion was not good. He considered himself a great gourmet, but I cannot say he showed any knowledge of good cooking. I once heard him talking to an acquaintance and discussing a third party, and he wound up his description by saying, " I tell you what he is like ; he is the sort of man who eats marmalade for breakfast ". I asked him afterwards what he considered to be a perfect breakfast, and he replied, " A bottle of fresh strawberries and a pint of champagne ". He had (so far as I could judge) no intellectual tastes, but he was fond of music and could amuse himself for an hour or so at the piano, though he was not a musician.

At Sydney we were put up at Government House. Sir Hercules Robinson was Governor, and he and Lady Robinson had known Cairns in Ceylon ; but they evidently did not think much of each other, and Cairns never hid from me his dislike of Lady Robinson. I found my old school and college friend, Walter Hely Hutchinson,[1] installed as Private Secretary to Sir Hercules.

I think we stayed three days. And the third day some people had been asked to meet us at dinner, but that day Cairns said that we must get on our way, and we went on board the *Barracouta* that afternoon, but we did not start ! For Captain Stevens had been asked to the dinner at Government House, and had no intention of getting under way until next day. Cairns did not seem to mind the delay,

---

[1] Later the Rt. Hon. Sir Walter Hely Hutchinson, P.C., G.C.M.G., Governor of the Cape of Good Hope.

58

as long as he could get away from Government House and Lady Robinson.

I had my negro boy whom I had engaged in Trinidad. Cairns had picked up two youths, who were stewards on board one of the P. & O. ships, on our way to Melbourne; and now he told one of them to open his uniform case, as he must wear uniform on landing. What was his horror to find that all the gold oak-leaves on one side of his first-class Civil Service uniform had turned black. At luncheon that day he told his woes to Captain Stevens, who said, " That can be put all right. We have a first-rate fellow on board who looks after all the gold on our uniforms; he will attend to it for you ". So it was handed over to the expert, with the result that he removed the black, but also removed all the gilding with it, so that one side remained gold and the other side silver.

I was told afterwards that Captain Stevens' orders were to take us to the mouth of the Brisbane river and no further, but this did not suit him at all, and he steamed up the river and dropped anchor opposite Government House. Then we landed, and the *Barracouta* fired a salute, shaking all the windows in the town.

We were met by a deputation on the landing stage, and then entered carriages and were driven all round the town to Government House. It was a terrifically hot day, and as we were all in uniform and cocked hats the heat was almost unbearable. At the house we were met by the Chief Justice and the Cabinet, and many others, and the Governor was sworn in.

The Chief Justice read the Commission, which I handed to him with the seal attached, in a tin case. Then he told me to display the seal, and I hinted to him that it was not advisable ; but he insisted, and when the case was opened a shower of wax powder spread over the table and only a small portion of the seal still adhered to the silk card. I knew the seal was all broken in pieces, but the Chief Justice would not take my word for it. At last we got rid of our visitors, and H. E., Captain Stevens, MacCarthy and I sat round the table in our shirt-sleeves and tried to get cool, and asked for something to drink ; but there was absolutely nothing to drink in the house, and we had to send an orderly to the nearest bar for refreshments.

Government House was quite a good building, standing in a garden which joined the Botanical Garden, but the house was rather scantily furnished, and I did not find it very easy to get all I needed. This amused me, as in Trinidad, when I asked for anything for Government House, I was always referred to the Queensland Act, which was held to be a model in such matters.

CHAPTER VI

QUEENSLAND

A few days after our arrival we were taken by train up to Toowomba to an agricultural show. A barouche and a pair of horses met us at the station, and after going round the show we were given lunch. A big man, who had evidently had enough to drink, sat down opposite to Captain Stevens, who had come up with us, and opened the conversation in a loud voice across the table by saying, " You are a Captain of a man-of-war, aren't you ? What's your screw ? I suppose they give you about as much as I give my groom ? " I asked who he was, and was inclined to resent his rudeness, but was told that he was known as the King of Toowomba, and that we were practically his guests, as the carriage we were using was his !

We were taken to a big dinner that night, and after the usual toasts the speeches began to tend towards local politics, upon which the Governor suddenly got up and bolted, and went out by a back door. As his sight was not good, and it was very dark, I had some difficulty in extracting him, in a very bad temper, from what appeared to be a rubbish heap. Perhaps it was as well that he

61

cleared out, for the diners evidently made a night of it, and it was a very chippy lot of Cabinet Ministers who joined us next morning in the train.

In a few days our heavy baggage arrived, and the servants whom Cairns had engaged in England. They were all boys, or very youthful, and not up to their work. Then there was a French cook, whom Cairns had engaged from the Café Anglais in Paris, who was certainly a duffer. No woman was allowed in the house! We usually went for solemn drives for an hour or so in the afternoon, and once or twice for equally solemn rides in the morning. The visits to the various offices and Government establishments were sometimes interesting.

As Cairns disliked MacCarthy and hated being left alone with him, I was nearly always in attendance. I had a sort of Assistant Secretary in Albert Drury, who came every day. He had held that position with three or four Governors, and was my source of information in all local matters. As he sat in my office copying despatches he used to go through all his past experiences, and I heard many amusing stories of Gubernatorial doings, but if I made a comment or asked a question he seemed suddenly to think he was indiscreet, and dried up at once, so I learnt to let him yarn on without interruption.

The Governor was fond of giving dances, and the Hall made an excellent ballroom, as the floor was laid with narrow planks length-wise, like a ship's deck, and had a capital surface. It did not take long to decorate the house, as I sent an orderly out into the bush early in the morning, and he would bring me a great truss of magnificent long-stemmed maiden-hair fern, and I could cut two hundred big heads of scarlet *Poinsettia* in the garden without their being missed. Supper and all arrangements were entrusted to the local Gunter. The first dance we gave was not altogether a success, as we had, in our ignorance of local conditions, asked a good many people who were not on friendly terms. As I did not know the guests well enough to venture on any introductions, the only thing to do was to dance every dance myself and make MacCarthy do the same. I did miss one dance, when I escaped to my room to make a complete change, for it was the middle of the hot weather and I was wet through!

In March I wrote a letter to my brother, in which I said, " I have now been here nearly two months, and that, added to the time spent with the Governor on the way to Australia, is long enough to form a pretty good idea of how I shall get on with him, and what sort of life I shall lead here, and I cannot report favourably. As MacCarthy and I are the Governor's only companions, and he hates being alone when not in his office, we have plenty of his society, and it is not of the liveliest description. When he is in a good temper he can be pleasant enough, but one never knows how long it will last, and our meals are often too dismal. I used to force conversation at first, but he was such a wet blanket that I have given it up, and eat too much in consequence.

"Sometimes the Governor goes out at three o'clock in a carriage to visit some institution, and one of us goes with him, but often he won't stir out until five o'clock. I don't care much for driving along the same roads (and there are very few of them), and a walk is as bad, since it only means pottering about the Botanical Gardens, as he will not go outside the gate, because of passing through the town.

"We dine at eight, and afterwards go into the drawing-room, where Cairns will sometimes play for a little on the piano, or we play dummy whist or dominoes for about half an hour—when H. E. usually falls asleep, and as soon after ten as he happens to awake we all go to bed. Altogether not a very interesting day.

"Many of the people who come to call upon the Governor leave cards on me, but H. E. asked me only to leave cards in return, and not to go to their houses; and when the Committee of the Brisbane Club made us honorary members, he asked us never to go near the place. It is all too ludicrous."

Things did not improve, and on the 10th April I wrote a formal letter to Cairns, asking him to look out for someone to take my place, on the grounds that I had been used to a more active life, and felt the restraint more than I had anticipated. He took my action more quietly than I expected, and after talking the matter over it was agreed that I should give it a further trial for six weeks or two months.

However, the household was more chaotic than

ever, and I cannot do better than transcribe a letter I wrote at this time to my sister, which I asked her to treat as confidential, for both MacCarthy and myself were very anxious not to give the show away, although we found it very difficult to avoid the inquisitiveness of local gossips.

Letter to my sister,

"I really must give you in detail the state of the establishment. Of the five men who came out in the *Abbey Holme* three, including the butler, have already been discharged; they really were a bad lot. There remains Thomas, aged twenty-two years, the coachman, who drives very badly and is to leave at the end of the month, and the black boy from Trinidad. Two men (stewards) were taken from the P. & O. Steamer *Pera*; one, a scoundrel, has been sacked, and the other, Roberts, has been promoted to be House Steward. He is about twenty-four years old, pushing, rather impudent, and with a queer temper; has taken an oath never to touch liquor, and has now been given by the Governor complete charge of the household, though the other servants dislike him. Next comes Hopper, a nice youth, age twenty-one, who comes from the Thatched House Club, of which the Governor is a member. He came out intending to go up-country, but was captured on landing and taken into the household. He is a very good fellow, but knows nothing about waiting or housework. Next on the list is a youth about twenty, a complete country lout, who has

65

been put into black clothes and attempts to wait at table (he was caught fresh from the last emigrant ship); and last a boy, also from an emigrant ship, who helps to scrub in the kitchen. Cook we have none (the French cook has gone); the wife of another emigrant (who had been put to work in the stables although he had never touched a horse before) ruins a leg of mutton or a joint of beef in her attempts to prepare them for our dinner. The beefsteak she cooked for breakfast to-day was very cold when it came to table, and on inquiry we were told that it had been found necessary to wash it before bringing it in!

"The boy who attends to my bedroom, when he has time, yesterday made out that he was ill, and when I went up to bed at ten o'clock I found that my room had not been touched all day, and I had to make the bed myself. And this is Vice-Regal life!

"Now about the stable! You would think that there would be no difficulty about buying horses in Australia. Well, there is hardly a decent carriage-horse to be got in the place. The Chief of the Police, Captain Seymour, did succeed in picking up one fair pair in Brisbane, but nearly the first day the Governor went for a drive they had their necks rubbed by collars and had to be rested for a week. Then when put into harness again one of them refused to move; he jibbed over and over again, and yesterday afternoon it was found impossible to get him out of the stable yard. The coach-boy

(I cannot call him a coachman) is a duffer, loses his temper and uses his whip. He shan't drive them again if I can help it. Then I had them driven by a livery-stable keeper in the town, a first-rate whip, and he had very little trouble with them.

"Now for another horse incident. Captain Seymour told a certain Mr M——, a very good judge, to pick up some horses for the Governor in New South Wales or Tasmania, where he was travelling. Telegrams kept flying about from M—— to say he had bought a splendid pair and had sent them off from Tasmania, a thousand miles by sea, and had bought six hacks, which was more than he was asked for. When a message reached him to say that it was more than were wanted he was indignant, and kept sending poor Seymour telegrams of an extraordinary and insulting nature.

"In time the Tasmanian carriage horses arrived; he had paid one hundred and fifty guineas for them, and on inspection they proved to be perfect screws worth about twenty pounds the pair. All this time a perfect war of telegraphic messages was flying between Seymour and M—— about the hacks.

"Now at last it has turned out that M—— has gone out of his mind, and some of his relations have gone to look after him. He has been throwing away his money buying horses and cattle right and left. It appears he had sunstroke in India, and lately has been dissipating a good deal, and that has completely finished him up. Of course the carriage-horses have gone back, and the matter is being made the best of by Seymour, who has all through the difficulty behaved very well indeed.

"Now for one more bit of bad luck and I won't trouble you with my woes any more. Two really nice horses were picked up by the buyer for the police. The Governor, who knows nothing whatever about horses and can't ride a bit, went out on the gray once or twice and seemed to like him. The brown horse, nearly a thoroughbred, I rode the day he arrived and liked it very much. Well, last Thursday, the Governor was to have gone out in the carriage, but the horses would not move from the front door, and eventually had to be led back to the stable. Then the Governor told Hopper, whom he believed to be a good horseman, to take the brown horse out for exercise. In about half an hour Hopper came back to say the horse was so restive it was impossible to mount him. Then said the Governor, 'Take out the gray', which he did, and then I saw what was the matter. Hopper could not ride a little bit. I told the Governor this, who replied that he did not know what to do, that he could not manage the stable, and that he would give it all over to me! A nice little job. A useless boy as a coachman, and a helper who had been only a week with horses; carriage horses that jibbed, and two fine hacks that the Governor was really afraid of riding.

"I thought it best to exercise the hacks myself, and not let them eat their heads off in the stable. The brown would make a capital hack for the Governor but I hardly think I shall get him on horseback again.

68

". . . I must add one more servant story. The immaculate Roberts whom the Governor petted and made much of, and for whom the doctor was sent for because he suffered from hysteria, has at last been found out. It was drink all the time. Now we have arrived at the very depths we cannot possibly become worse off than we are now. A female cook is coming up from Melbourne soon. I wish her a quick voyage. I am told she cooks well, but I know she drinks. Well, beggars must not be choosers."

. . . . .

1st May.—" Last night we gave our second dance, It went off much better than the first, and we had really quite a pleasant evening.

". . . Last Thursday Parliament met, and we went down in state to open it. Guard of honour, of the Volunteers, police guard, and our two mounted orderlies smartened up for the occasion, and of course full uniform for ourselves. My chief difficulty was the coachman and horses, as our coach-boy had been sacked, and the livery, which had been made to fit him, was very small, and the horses were not dependable on account of their jibbing. However, I put one of our own horses in and borrowed another, a very fair match, and then came the question of livery for the coachman, a man from a livery stable in the town, known as Jerry. I managed to squeeze him into the coat and breeches, but the hat and boots were hopeless. I brushed up an old black hat of my own, and lent him a pair of my own black boots, and put on them a very seedy pair of brown tops, borrowed from a coachman in the town, and made him, I hope, look decent in the not very critical eyes of a Brisbane crowd.

"It was only at almost the last moment that I was allowed to put Jerry into livery at all, the Governor wanting him to drive in his very seedy blue coat with silver buttons that he uses when he drives the flies in the town, but I really could not stand that."

.   .   .   .   .

"A few days later we paid a visit to Ipswich for the Agricultural Show, and our reception was not very flattering.   Nothing actually went wrong, but the Ipswich people were put out at H. E. only coming up for the day, and not attending the dinner or the ball, and they did not forget to let him know what they thought of it.

"Next morning Mr Walsh, the Speaker of the House (who is a gentleman and a man of the world), called in the morning, and had a long talk with the Governor, and I fancy must have pitched into him pretty strongly, for the upshot of it all is that the Governor has asked MacCarthy and me to go occasionally to the Club, and to make the acquaintance of some of the people there, and also asked me to attend the debates in the House.   (When I told him last week that I had been to hear the debate on the Address he forbade my going there again.)   Mr Walsh must have told him some of the stories which are going all over the town, and I think he must now feel what a stupid mistake he has been making all this time. We have come down to women servants at last, a cook and a housemaid, who arrived an hour ago, and we now get something to eat."

I had frequently to go to the House in uniform to present messages from the Governor or Bills signed by him ; and had to make all the conventional bows and hand my paper to the Speaker, and then go out backwards all the way down the House, making my bows again, which I somehow managed to do without tripping over my sword or kicking the members' legs.

News came to us that Sir Arthur and Lady Gordon, with Miss Gordon Cumming and Sir Arthur's staff, were arriving from England by way of Singapore and Torres Straits on their way to Fiji, and would be in Brisbane for a day ; and of course the Governor had to ask them to stay at Government House. However, H. E. told me that he would put up Sir Arthur and the ladies, but refused to put the staff up ; and said I must find them accommodation elsewhere. This I found impossible, as Government House was outside the town, Parliament was sitting, and the town was full up. So when they arrived I told Arthur Gordon, the Private Secretary, and Captain Knollys, the A.D.C., of my difficulty, and asked them if they would mind shake-downs in my bedroom, which was a large room and away from the other part of the house. This they agreed to, and I said nothing to the Governor about it.

My difficulty all along had been with the servants. These wretched youths quarrelled, sometimes got drunk, and were generally a nuisance. The best of them, who was only about twenty-two, fell ill and died; and Cairns took the opportunity of sending me verses he had composed on the event. Things had come to a climax when the Gordons arrived, for with the exception of the black boy all the men-servants went on strike, and refused to work (this was before the French cook had left, and I kept him in the kitchen with some outside help). We had asked the Speaker, the Prime Minister, and other principal people to dinner to meet the Gordons ! Abbey, Sir Arthur's house steward, would keep loafing round, and I did my best to persuade him to go and see the sights in the town. Had I known him as well as I did later on, I should have asked him to lend a hand. I was told afterwards that he said to Captain Knollys, " This is a rum Government House, Sir. I have just seen the Private Secretary laying the table for dinner ".

By dinner-time I had managed to persuade some of the servants to resume work, and the dinner was fairly well served.

That night, when we got to my bedroom, I told Knollys and Arthur Gordon that I should be leaving soon, and would very likely pay them a visit in Fiji on my way home. This they must afterwards have told to Sir Arthur; for he wrote to Cairns from Sydney, and at the end of his letter said that if he (Cairns) could spare me, he would be very glad of my services, as he would have a great deal to do when he arrived in Fiji, and was very short-handed. As I had already written formally to Cairns asking him to look for some one to take my place, since I found the life so unsuitable, this letter enabled him to gazette me as going on special duty to Fiji, thus avoiding all question of why I was leaving.

I must say that the last two months of my stay in Queensland were very much pleasanter, and I found the people both agreeable and hospitable. Things had gone much better since I had told the Governor of my intention of leaving him.

CHAPTER VII

SYDNEY AND FIJI

At the end of July I took passage in the ss. *Governor Blackhall*. On our way down the coast the Captain strolled up to me on deck and said, " Mr Maudslay, are you fond of fishing ? " I said, " Yes", and he replied, " Let us stop and do a little fishing". As soon as the engines slowed down, fishing lines appeared by magic, and I never saw so many fish caught in so short a time—great big red snappers ; but an old lady, who overheard my conversation with the Captain, was furious and marched up and down the deck, asking if anyone had ever heard of such a disgraceful thing as stopping a steamer carrying Her Majesty's Mails to indulge in a little fishing. Of course it was all a put-up job. The Captain knew he had an hour or two to spare in order to make Sydney Heads in daylight, and he knew his fishing ground. But the old lady was not to be appeased, until dinner-time came, when she could not resist a helping of fresh fish, but before eating it she left her seat and walked up to the end of the table where the Captain was sitting, and made a formal apology.

At Sydney I found Lady Gordon and her two children Nevil and Jack, and some of the Fiji party.

74

Sir Arthur had already sailed with Commodore Goodenough in H.M.S. *Pearl,* and some of the others had gone ahead in another steamer. I had taken my passage in the *James Paterson,* sailing on the 7th August, but Lady Gordon asked me to delay my departure for a month and go with her and the children, and to this I consented.

Ristori was playing at the Sydney Theatre, and I had the good luck to see her both as Queen Elizabeth and as Marie Stuart. I was a good deal at Government House, and then went for a trip with Miss Ika Gordon Cumming into the Blue Mountains, where she made sketches of the "Weather Board" and other celebrated views. She had a distinct talent for landscape on a large scale, and after the first few hours' work on the spot the pictures were admirable. I think the only charm of a blue gum is the wonderful purples they give to the distant hills when clothed with them.

While we were away, we heard that the *Pearl* had come into Sydney Harbour with her yards scandalized, bringing home the dead body of Commodore Goodenough, who had been killed by natives in the Santa Crus Islands. I had been lunching with Mrs Goodenough only a few days before starting on my trip. It was of course an awful blow to her and to the Gordons.

The scene on the quarter deck when the Commodore knew he was dying, and bid good-bye to his officers and crew, had been most touching, for they all adored him, as it seemed did all who knew him.

75

After our trip to the Blue Mountains I went with Miss Gordon Cumming to stay with the Campbells at Duntroon. This was rather the show station and was quite comfortable and civilized, and the horses they gave one to ride were well broken. While we were staying there the Campbells gave a ball. All the ladies came on horseback, and after taking off coverings, shook out their flounces and put on their dancing shoes. We had to go on dancing until four o'clock, when the moon rose and the guests could see to ride home. One little thought at the time that Duntroon would be chosen as the site of the Capital of Australia and be now called Cambera.

There was a big race meeting at Flamstead when I got back to Sydney, and Sir Hercules gave me a seat on his coach each day; for he drove a very well-turned-out four-in-hand. His horse, Kingsborough, was the favourite for the big race, and lady Bob had made great preparation. A large box had lately arrived from Paris with a new frock in her husband's racing colours, broad red and white stripes, with bonnet and parasol to match. Lady Bob, who was the daughter of Lord Valentia, is a very voluminous lady, although I have been told that when Herky, then a cornet in a cavalry regiment carried her off, she was slim, and the best woman rider across country in Ireland. The sporting instinct was still strong. I was sitting behind her in the royal box next to her daughter when the big race was run. When Kingsborough came into the straight Lady Bob could not contain herself. She jumped up, waving her brilliant parasol over the front of the box, and shouting at the top of her voice, " Kingsborough wins ! Kingsborough wins ! " Her daughter kept on saying to me, " Mr Maudslay, do pull mother down ". Sir Hercules, knowing perhaps what her excitement would be, had discreetly retired to the Jockey Club Stand. I think the Royal Box attracted almost as much attention as the finish itself. Kingsborough pulled it off all right.

There is always a great rivalry between Sydney and Melbourne. Of course the Robinsons, like everyone else, go to Melbourne to see the race for the Melbourne Cup. I was told that the year before, some Melbourne lady, wishing to be polite to her, said, " I hope, Lady Robinson, we shall see you and Sir Hercules here some day ". Lady Bob pulled herself up and replied, " When Sir Hercules leaves Sydney, he looks for promotion ".

On the 9th September, 1875, we sailed in the ss. *Egmont* for Fiji. Our party included Lady Gordon and her two children Nevil and Jack, aged seven and five, and two nurses, Miss (Ika) Gordon Cumming, three Royal Engineer officers, Colonel Pratt, Captain Stewart and Lieutenant Lake, Dr Carew and a small party of R.E.'s; and among our fellow passengers were the Rev. F. Langham, the head of the Wesleyan Mission, and his wife, and a Mr Woods, late Prime Minister of Fiji, with whom I shared a cabin.

Previous to annexation Fiji had been rather unsuccessfully ruled by a mixed Government of whites and natives; Thacombau, the War Chief

77

(Vuni Valu) of Bau, had been the nominal king.
Mr Woods and Mr Thurston [1] had been members
of the Government. There were many stories current
of the doings of this Government. The Government
had decreed that Thacombau must have his portrait
painted as king, and I have seen this wonderful oil
colour hanging in Mr Thurston's house. The really
dignified old chieftain was supplied with a purple
velvet knickerbocker suit and a tall white hat, in
which to be painted. I wonder what has become
of that work of art. When the first proclamations
were issued by Mr Woods, they were headed Io!
Io! Io! When Woods was asked the reason, he
said, "Does not the crier at home cry,' Oh yes!
Oh yes!'? and that is the Fijian translation."

Treasury notes were issued by the Government,
but instead of the usual formula "On demand
I promise to pay", the notes bore the words, "The
bearer is entitled to receive". These notes were
cashed at the Treasury for a short time, but then
the Treasury ran dry, and when a note was presented
Woods, in his blandest manner, said, "We quite
agree that you are entitled to receive cash for that
note, but unfortunately just at the present the
Government is short of cash. You will notice there
is no promise to pay".

There was another story about the postage stamps.
The Government had made use of an old issue of
English stamps on which the letters C.R. had been

---

[1] Later on Sir John Thurston, K.C.M.G., High Commissioner
for the Western Pacific.

imprinted. I must explain that when a printing press had been set up by the Wesleyan Missionaries it was found that in printing Fijian the letters *t* and *h* were soon exhausted, and there was nothing to represent the frequent occurrence of *th*, but the letter *c* was not used at all; so they used it in place of *th*, and Thacombaus name was always written Cakobau, an m always being inserted in speaking before the *b*.

Woods was reported to have arrived at a Cabinet Council, and have asked angrily why the C.R. standing for Cakobau Rex had been printed on the stamps, adding that although he was Prime Minister to King Cakobau he was still a loyal British Subject, and he could see no reason why Cakobau should take her Majesty the Queen's family name. When pressed for his meaning he said, " Was not her Majesty's Uncle Georgius Rex ? "

It took us ten days to reach Fiji, and we approached Levuka in a heavy rainstorm. When the tumbled mass of mountains came into view as the rain cleared off I remember one of the engineers standing by me exclaiming, " My word ! are we expected to survey that ? " We were soon carried off in a boat and landed at Nasova, the Government House, about three quarters of a mile to the south of the town.

The town of Levuka, which was then the capital of Fiji, is situated on the east side of the Island of Ovalau on a narrow strip between the precipitous mountains and the sea. When Commodore

Goodenough on his return to Sydney had been asked what he thought of Levuka, he is reported to have replied that " It was a very nice place, there was only one road, and that was the beach, and the beach was made of broken gin bottles and the houses were built of the cases ".

This was a little hard on a very picturesque place, but one certainly totally unsuited for a metropolis.

To save repetition I will insert here a letter written to my sister about a year later—

" Both you and the mother ask me the same questions in the last letters I have received :—Why don't you tell me all about your daily life ? What sort of people you are living with, and what are your daily occupations ? So I suppose I must tell you, as well as I can, all about it, though it will probably bore you. To begin at the beginning. I suppose you know that Ovalau is an island, and that it is a very hilly one—that there are no roads, only native tracks, along which it is almost always necessary to walk in single file. Roughly speaking, the Island is oval in shape and about twelve miles long. There is a pretty good track round it, but you cannot walk much more than a mile without crossing a stream, and most likely the only bridge will be a single cocoa-nut log, perhaps about thirty or forty feet long.

" There are several tracks across the Island, all very rough walking. The coast is indented with many little bays, most of them with native villages close to the stream that runs down from the mountains. Nowhere is there any extent of flat land, and the hills are very rocky and precipitous. Levuka is built right on the shore, stretching back as far as there is any flat land, and on to the hills behind. Some of the shops are pretty good—the regular colonial store. The houses are most of them poor-looking wooden shanties. The roads about the town are a little better than the ordinary native tracks, but not much better. There are no wheeled carriages of any sort, and only a few horses. We have three ponies at Nasova, on which we sometimes ride to town, and sometimes into the country, but not often, as the tracks are so bad.

" Nasova, one might say, joins Levuka, as there are some houses all the way along the shore, but there is a point running out between the two, and you cannot see much of the one from the other. I look upon it as about three quarters of a mile's walk into town. Nasova consists only of Government House and a few of the public offices and their surroundings, a little guard-house, etc. A broad verandah runs round the house in every direction. Of course the verandah acts as a passage. The house is built of reeds, tied together with sinnet and fixed into a wooden framework. Rooms are divided off by no more than partitions about ten feet high, only the two centre bedrooms are boarded up to the the roof. So it wants no shouting to carry on a conversation with your next-door neighbour. On the whole the house is exceedingly comfortable, though you may hardly think so from the description. The floors are covered with mats.

"Now for the people. Our party consists in all of the Governor, Lady Gordon, two children, Jack and Nevil, Miss Gordon Cumming, Arthur Gordon (Private Secretary), Captain Knollys, A.D.C., Baron A. Von Hugel, a visitor, and Mr Le Hunte,[1] now a Stipendiary Magistrate at Loma Loma.

"*The Governor.*—A short man, dark, not good-looking, careless of his appearance, short-sighted. As a boy and young man he was his father's greatest friend and companion, and was his private secretary when he was Prime Minister. I believe his father never went anywhere, never did anything without him. He was brought up at Haddo, the Scotch country seat (I believe an awfully dull place), and was never sent to school, but he took a degree at Cambridge. Of course, as his father's Private Secretary, he knew all the people of the day worth knowing, and knew as well as his father everything that was going on. He was Gladstone's Private Secretary when High Commissioner to the Ionian Isles, and has always remained on intimate terms with him. He was for a short time in Parliament, then Governor of New Brunswick, Trinidad, Mauritius, Fiji. Nowhere has he been popular, since he has a very bad manner with strangers, and he is perfectly aware of it and regrets it much. He is very determined, and puts aside all opposition when his

[1] Later Sir George Le Hunte, G.C.M.G., Governor of Trinidad, etc.

82

mind is made up, but with people with whom he is in sympathy, though not agreeing, he is perfectly open to discussion, and even diffident to subordinates. His personal staff have always been strongly attached to him; with them he is always on the most perfectly easy terms, and not in the least exacting. He is a high Churchman with strong religious opinions which he does not air. He professes to be a thorough liberal, but his aristocratic leanings come out insensibly. He is very proud of his family and descent. He is very large-minded, and in some things almost an enthusiast. Well read, particularly in history and in some curiously odd subjects. Very fond of nature and scenery, he has a very artistic appreciation of light and colour. Active, a good walker, utterly careless of what he eats and drinks—or rather, I don't believe he ever knows what he eats and drinks. Often very preoccupied when there are difficult matters to settle or schemes to devise, he has a dreadful habit of putting off all writing until the last minute.

"Lady Gordon is a handsome woman. I would trust anything to her perfectly good sound sense and tact. I have never seen her in the least out of temper, and she is on the best of terms with the whole household. She dresses simply but very well, but the more she is dressed the better she looks. I like her immensely; we have been together a great deal, and have always been the best of friends. She always makes the best of things, and is luckily not nervous. Of course it is a very dull life for her here, as she is very fond of society. She has always been a very bad walker, and here she is without carriage or horses, and even the paths are hardly fit to walk upon, and an afternoon row inside the reef grows monotonous. Lady Gordon has the most implicit faith in the Governor, but is perfectly conscious of his little weak points and is very good-natured and good-humoured about them. I don't think Lady Gordon will be sorry when H. E.'s term of Government is over, and would be glad if he were not to accept another Government. The ladies of Levuka don't afford her any companions; they are certainly *not* first-class. Lady Gordon is a daughter of Sir John Shaw Lefevre ; she is not musical ; has a very great talent for drawing from model (not from life), which she hardly ever exercises.

"The children are Nevil, aged seven, and Jack, five. I am very fond of them. Nevil is particularly devoted to me, and Jack is very great fun, such a jolly boy.

"Miss Gordon Cumming (usually called by outsiders Miss Cummins, which annoys her) is a very tall, plain woman, a regular globe-trotter, wonderfully good-tempered, no tact, very pushing when she wants anything done, and yet one of the best-natured creatures in the world, and when anyone is ill or wants help I believe would go any distance out of her way to help them. She is sufficiently clothed in suits of brown holland or blue serge and wears an enormous pith hat. Her ' tavi ', as we say here, is to wander about the world and ' see things and paint them '. She has written a book of travels

in two large volumes which have been on the table
for a long time, but I have not read them. She can
write fluently and well, and describes the things
that she actually sees very clearly, but when she
goes beyond that, and flies much higher, she fails.
Her talent for water-colour drawing is a curious one.
She has had very little instruction, yet no subject
is too big for her; the larger and more imposing
it is the better she likes it. She sketches in her outline with the most wonderful rapidity and accuracy,
and when her pictures are about three parts done
they are often most admirable but she persists in
taking them home to finish them, and that takes
away much of their merit. She had the other day
two sketches taken on the Upper Rewa that I would
have given her anything for, as they were when
she left off sketching on the spot, but she must needs
finish them at home and now they have lost their
charm. I am afraid we all tease the poor woman
a good deal, but then she does rise so beautifully,
and besides is quite capable of taking care of herself.
Missionaries are a fine bait. She travels about the
country a good deal with the Missionaries, and is
given to looking at things not only from their point of
view, but from the ideas they have crammed her
with. I believe she has written some articles for
Good Words on Fiji, but they have not yet been
printed. I think she is absolutely frightened to
write a book on Fiji,[1] which is a great relief.

[1] She wrote, *At Home in Fiji*, two vols. Blackwood & Sons, 1881.

" I never found her so agreeable as when we were for a week together in a lonely hotel in the Blue Mountains of New South Wales. She is off now on a trip to Windward in the Missionary schooner. Miss G. C. is no relation whatever of the Governor, she merely came out as a friend, and I don't think Lady G. knew much of her until they met on board ship.

" *Arthur Gordon*, Private Secretary. A short, good-looking or rather picturesque-looking man, wiry and athletic, swims, walks, dances, paints and draws most admirably ; hates his Private Secretary's work, in fact never does it. He is a very distant relation of the Governor ; he joined the Governor when he was about sixteen years old. (H. E. was then Governor of New Brunswick), and since then has never left him ; he has always nominally been his Private Secretary, and as long as there were plenty of clerks to do the work it suited him very well. H. E. always owns to me that he knows he spoils him dreadfully, and there is no doubt that he does. Since I have been here I have done the whole of his work, and he has amused himself going about the country. Lately he has had command of a large body of natives, fighting the Kai Colo, and has done his work most admirably. We are always on very good terms, but I don't think I will say anything more about him, for in reality we are not in the least in sympathy with one another. He is more often away from Nasova than he is here.

" *Captain Knollys*, *A.D.C.* A very good line officer

who thinks the 32nd Light Infantry the finest regiment in the world. He is delightfully pig-headed and dogmatic, and is very fond of arguing. He is a first-rate fellow, however, with lots of common sense. He has also been for some time acting Superintendent of the Police. Lately he has had command of the Police in the Mountains, and has managed very well indeed. He does his A.D.C.'s work satisfactorily, but with Abbey the steward to manage the house that does not come to much.

"*Baron Anatole Von Hügel* was a visitor. He had come from New Zealand a month or two earlier, and had gone to Viti Levu hunting for native weapons, etc., for he was a keen collector. His father, who had been Austrian Minister in Belgium, had been a well-known traveller, and his mother was Scotch. Arthur Gordon had met him up in the mountains of Viti Levu (where he was half starved on native food, had spent all his money, and had even cut the buttons off his clothes in exchange for native orna-ments), and had brought him back to Nasova. The native women and children adored him, and he always reminded me of the Pied Piper when one saw him in a native village with all the children hanging on to him. He was about twenty years old and a most delightful companion. He had come from New Zealand in the Wesleyan Missionary ship, and as he was a Roman Catholic had not been very favourably treated by his fellow passengers; and one of my first jobs was to smooth out a dispute which had arisen between them.

"The Baron's bedroom was next to mine, and as he would sit up very late writing letters and notes on native customs I usually got him out of bed in the morning with the aid of a native fish spear which was easily passed through the reed partition between our rooms. Then we all went off to bathe from the jetty in front of the house.

"We have such a number of pets about the house. Our two beautiful green and blue parrots, I am sorry to say, have disappeared, but we have a white and saffron cockatoo from the Solomon Islands, and a blue and claret-coloured parrot, most beautifully and strangely marked, but very savage; two laughing jackasses from Australia, and one little blue and white kingfisher that had hardly any feathers on when brought to the house, he was so very young. His parents used to come down every morning and evening from the woods to pay him a visit, but he never tried to get away, and has grown up quite strong and devours a number of cockroaches nightly, running about the pantry and attacking every cockroach that dares to shew its face. He nearly came to an untimely end the other day, for one of the jackasses was detected in the act of swallowing him, and he was just pulled out in time by one of the servants. It was an act of the purest cannibalism on the part of the jackass, as he and the kingfisher belong to the same tribe. My greatest pet is a little lorikeet about the size of a bullfinch; his back and tail are the most beautiful golden green, his breast and the ring round his neck are a bright crimson, and his head and the feathers round his legs are purple. You cannot imagine anything more lovely. There is nothing of the vulgarity of a gaudy-coloured parrot about him, and he has a pretty little beak and a long brush tongue. He is perfectly tame and likes to sit upon my head and pass his feather tongue along a single hair. He lives just outside my bedroom and his favourite perch is on the branch of a brilliant yellow croton, which suits his style of beauty exactly."

CHAPTER VIII

FIJI

It was indeed a great change from life in Brisbane. Here all was stir and activity. I was at first only a guest, but I lent a hand in all that was going on. The first few weeks I was chiefly engaged in helping Lady Gordon to get the house into something like order. Abbey, the steward, and his wife were untiring workers in getting things put straight and training native servants, no easy job. We saw a good deal of the native chiefs, who often came to lunch or dinner, and even those who had never eaten at a white man's table before always showed perfectly good manners.

I think the Governor's staff stood somewhat in awe of him, but I got on with him very well indeed, and we were much together, walking, boating, and bathing. As young Arthur Gordon was often away travelling in Viti Levu, the big island, and Le Hunte went off to do Magistrate's work in the Eastern Islands, most of the Private Secretary's work fell to my lot. The Governor had an uncomfortable habit of jotting down paragraphs of despatches or other business memoranda on the backs of old envelopes or any other scraps of paper he could put his hands on, and this made the copying of despatches, etc., often tedious work, and his table was usually heaped up with documents. I was told by the others that it was as much as one's life was worth to touch the Governor's papers; but the first time he went away for a few days I thoroughly cleared up his room, put all the papers in order, destroyed all old envelopes and scraps of paper, and placed half-sheets tied together at the corner with conspicuous red silk ribbon on his office table and in all other places he was likely to sit down to write; and when he returned not a word of complaint was raised, and I never had any further trouble about missing paragraphs of a despatch. But he never could be got to be forehanded in writing. When anxious officials were asking for him, he would be up in the drawing-room building brick castles with the children; but I know that all the time he was working out in his mind what he had to say, and all his best despatches were written under press of time, but it involved our sitting up half the night copying, docketing, etc., on mail-nights.

So far I had no official position. But about December, 1875, I was gazetted as Private Secretary and was put on the commission for settling pre-annexation debts, but I received no salary.

There was an English church in Levuka, but before I arrived the clergyman had been obliged to go to Australia; and before leaving he had arranged with the Government House staff to carry on the services during his absence. Of course I was called on to assist ; we wore surplices and took it in turn to read the service and preach. There was a book of Kingsley's sermons among the Governor's books, but by the time I was called on these were exhausted, so I preached two sermons, one on St. Francis of Assisi, and another on Ignatius Loyola, cribbed out of *Stephen's Lectures on Ecclesiastical History*. Putting an appropriate text in front, and prefacing with some remarks about living in the land of a successful Christian Mission, they went very well.

In December the weather began to get hot, and Dr MacGregor [1], our chief medical officer, was anxious to get the children out of Nasova for a time, so we went to Suva on Viti Levu, the big island, whence I wrote the following letter to my sister—

SUVA,
Sunday, 6th December.

" We came from Levuka in our new small steamer, the *Fitzroy*, and our party consists of the Governor, Lady Gordon, their two small children, Miss Gordon Cumming, a nurse, a native boat's crew and a few Indian and native servants. We are lodged in what is known as the Suva Hotel ! an uninhabited wooden shanty with an unlined tin roof ; and my first work was to send our four-oared gig up the bay to cut bundles of reeds with which to cover the roof, as heat under the tin was unbearable. Suva is the possible site of the future Capital, so we were all most anxious to see it. At present there is only one house here which is owned by a white family.

[1] Later the Rt. Hon. Sir William MacGregor, P.C., G.C.M.G., C.B., Governor of New Guinea, Lagos, Newfoundland, Queensland, etc.

92

The view over the bay is beautiful, and there is a splendid outline of mountains on the far side.

"We went to the native church this morning. Of course all sit on the floor, and when the natives pray they put their heads down on the mats; it looks so odd. The sermon was well delivered by the native teacher, his voice and gestures were both good, but he spoke so fast I could not understand much of it. When I asked what time the service was to be, I was told that it took place as soon as the tree in front of the teacher's house opened the last of its leaves! After service we went to look at the tree or rather shrub; it was a Bauhinia, and the leaves on the long branches unfold one by one, the end leaves opening last. When the end leaf opens the teacher reads morning prayers, and when the last leaf closes at night he reads evening prayers. We certainly made the most of our time while the Governor was staying here, and explored all the rivers and creeks which run into this beautiful bay. For the first half mile or so, and sometimes much further up, the rivers are fringed with a forest of mangrove, but not enough to make the colour monotonous, as in some of the West Indian rivers; then by degrees one gets into the regular forest-land of the tropics, with long lianes and festoons of creepers hanging from all the trees; the woods swarm with bright-coloured parrots, and there are more birds with pretty notes than I have ever heard in the tropics before, one with a song like our blackbird at home.

"We take our lunch with us and land to eat it on the banks of a stream, or in one of the queer little native villages. The houses are made on a framework of large half-trimmed timber, and the yellow reed walls are supported with pillars of black tree-fern stems. The inside of the high-pitched thatch roof is a beautiful bronze colour, from the smoke that curls up from the wood ashes in which most of the cooking is done. And the fireplace itself in the middle of the floor, with its four roughly-carved posts and round stones to support the great earthen cooking pots, is perhaps the most picturesque thing of all. The two shelves above the fireplace always hold curiously-shaped earthen vessels or wooden bowls; and hanging from the wall there is sure to be a bright-coloured *liku*[1] or a *sulu*[2] of tappa, or perhaps a bundle of white hibiscus fibre for straining *yangona* (*kava*)[3]. Sometimes one can spy, tied up to a post, a heavy war club, or half-hidden in the roof a beautifully carved spear.

"There are no windows, and all the light has to come through the low doorway; so it takes some minutes before one can make out the shape and use of the different objects. But it would need a Dutch artist to give you any idea of the quaint picturesqueness of the interior of a Fijian house.

"It is really most wonderful, the change that

---

[1] Liku, a short skirt made of strips of Pandanus leaves dyed red or yellow.

[2] Sulu, a skirt of native cloth made from the beaten-out bark of the paper mulberry.

[3] Yangona or kava, the root of Piper Methisticum.

in so few years has come over some of the natives.
The people just over the other side of the bay, not
twenty minutes' sail, were very dangerous to go
among two years ago. Now they are all (professed)
Christians, and send their children to school. And
one is as safe among them as one would be at home.
Some distance down the coast there is a little danger
still; and I was much amused at the district Magistrate telling me that at evening prayers, in a village
where he had lately been staying, the native teacher
offered up a prayer 'that he and his flock might
be granted strength to withstand the temptation
of clubbing the white man '.

"I came to Fiji rather prejudiced against the
missionaries, but am bound to own that the work
they have done is really wonderful. So far I have
been lucky in meeting the most favourable specimens,
and I believe that in Fiji the missionaries are of
a more modern school, and are more enlightened
and liberal in their ideas than are some in the islands
to the East; but, even here, they are too fond of
clothing the natives, and have yet a sneaking liking
for black coats.

"We went last Thursday with the Governor to
pay his first official visit to Rewa, rather a hard
pull in the gig against a strong head-wind. When
once we got into the river-mouth, or rather one of
the river-mouths, for there are many of them, the
change from the rugged mountain scenery we had
become used to was most complete. Considering
the size of the island of Viti Levu, the Rewa is

certainly a gigantic river ; the breadth close to Rewa Town is nearly that of the Thames at Westminster. The delta forms a large alluvial tract, thickly populated, and I should think very productive. A large number of natives were assembled on the bank when we landed, all of course squatting down in the attitude of respect, and a splendid *tama*[1] was given as H. E. stepped on shore. We now formed a good large party, as some of the staff had returned from the coast, and two boats with officers from H.M.S. *Nymphe* had come up the river to meet us. Lady Gordon went to stay at the Missionaries' house, and the Governor and all of us took possession of a large native house which had been cleared out for us. Soon after our arrival all the native aristocracy came to the house to drink yangona (kava) with the Governor. The drinking was of course done with full ceremonial, and the *tama* when H. E. drank was the best I have ever heard ; it is a combination of sounds quite impossible to describe.

" The programme for Friday was an examination of the school children, and then the Roko Tui Draketi, chief of the District, was to be sworn in and presented with his staff of office, to be followed by some *mékés* (native dances).

" Next morning, after a swim in the river, we went to look at the church, really a fine building, all native work, the walls of coral lime plaster, with a high pitched roof supported on two rows of fine wooden pillars. The end of the ridge pole, on the

---

[1] Tama, a curious guttural sound, given as a sign of respect.

outside, was ornamented with large white cowrie shells, generally used only to decorate the canoes of the chiefs. The ties of the beams inside are covered with plaited sinnet (cocoa-nut fibre) worked into attractive patterns in two or three colours.

" I spent the morning watching the country people coming into town with their smart dancing dresses tied up in bundles, some of them with their heads already painted and their hair done up in folds of tappa in the oddest way possible. All this time the *lalis* (wooden drums) had been making a great row in the *rara* (the open square or lawn in front of the church). When all the people were assembled we took our seats under a canopy of mats to screen us from the sun. The school children (it is hardly right to call them children, as many were quite grown up) were formed up in single file round the rara, and then passed one by one before the Governor, each reading a verse of the Bible. Nearly all of them read well, although some of them were very nervous. However, there were such a lot of them that after about two hundred and fifty of them had read, the others had to be passed by quickly in silence. Then some of them came up and wrote from dictation, and the performance was very creditable indeed. Then followed the school *méké*.[1] Each school retired a little in a body, and then all came towards us in a long line, moving in most perfect time and chanting as they came. The chant was a sort of Fijian version of

[1] Dance.

Nunc Dimittis; all the movements were perfect, and the way in which the tune, if one can call it such, was taken up a third lower by those behind was most effective. When they had come close enough to the Governor, at a signal from the teacher, they all sat down and began a geography lesson. The native teacher called out the name of a country, beginning with Britain, then in a low minor key one of the children began to chant Piritania sa Matanitu, Piritania sa Matanitu (Britain is a kingdom), and then a third higher, some other words giving Britain's position, and then with a swaying motion of their bodies and a rhythmical clapping of hands all joined in a chant of the extent, government etc., of the British Empire—in fact, a school geography lesson turned into a rather pretty song; and in this way went through all the principal countries of Europe.

"After the children had moved off, there came the ceremony of presenting the Roko Tui with his staff of office and a speech by the Governor. This was followed by what was the event of the day, the *mékés*. The first was to be one, not often given, known as the Flying Fox Dance.

"From the half-hidden roads leading into the *rara* on either side came two bands of men dressed in *licus* (sort of fringe petticoats) of green and coloured leaves, beautifully made, the leaves lying very thick one over the other and reaching below the knee. Such fine strapping men, many of them chiefs! Some had their faces blackened or painted black and red, and their heads done up in the most elaborate way with folds of fine white tappa. Garlands of flowers and leaves hung round their necks, and they wore armlets and garters of bright-coloured leaves on their arms and legs. To describe the dance to you is far beyond my powers; I can only give you the bare outline. The performers numbered about one hundred and twenty men and sixty children. The two parties approached one another in the usual *méké* form; it is an odd mixture of march, dance, and chant, and then after what seemed to be a consultation they agreed to rob a banana plant of its fruit. This plant, I must tell you, was tied to a pole in the middle of the *rara*, and had a large artificial fruit made of round nuts or gourds filled with oil, and a black square gin-bottle at the end of it, also full of oil, I believe, and not gin. After the consultation scouts were sent out from either party to see that all was safe, and they went flying round the square with their arms stretched out making a noise like the flying foxes. Then with a great deal of dancing the main bodies approached the tree and one of the foxes climbed up, while the little flying foxes circled round crying with delight at the sight of the fruit. The fox in the tree hung by his legs and flapped his arms and went into raptures of noisy delight over the feast; then another climbed up after him and they bit and scratched and squalled, just as the big bats do, and the first comer was turned out. All this time, of course, the dance was going on below. The time was wonderful,

99

every swish of their *licus* was in unison, and they were most clever in adapting themselves to any inequality in the ground. The musical accompaniment consisted of wooden drums and hollow bamboos drummed on the ground by about twenty gaily-dressed old gentlemen. The dance must have gone on for half an hour, with a slight pause at the end of each figure, when at last a man stepped out from the side, shot at the flying fox in the tree, who fell dead and the dance ended.

" The next was a club dance. I forgot to tell you that, except, on the Church side, the rara was surrounded by groves of banana and bread-fruit trees, so that one saw nothing of the preparations, forming in line, etc., and one heard the chants and shouts before the head of the war parties appeared. First came two parties each about seventy strong, marching three deep, armed with short spears of bamboo, cut into fantastic shapes at the end, the shafts painted and the handles covered with matting. As the two parties approached one another, they chanted and swung their bodies from side to side, thrusting and parrying with their spears, every hand and every foot moving together. When about twelve yards apart, each party wheeled away from us, and we saw approaching from a distance a body of men armed with clubs, every man in the front row with fine large breast ornaments of whales' teeth and pearl shell. The licus were even more brilliant than in the last dance, and the bodies and faces more elaborately painted in black and red;

some had large boar's teeth swung from their necks, and armlets, braces and garters of shell; others had long streamers of gauze-like tappa hanging from their heads, or wound in thick folds round the waist with long streamers behind; others had turbans of tappa dyed a bright blue, every man according to his fancy. The dance was wild and picturesque. There must have been two hundred and fifty of them, all fine, well-made fellows, and all chiefs or men of high birth. The old gentlemen of the orchestra never seemed to get tired, and kept up a loud strumming and wild chant all the time.

" The next dance was the most graceful of all. The dresses were much the same as before, with more gauzy white tappa, and some of the men from both the previous mêkês took part; and there were also a number of children with bright licus and garlands. The dance was called the ' Ua-loco-loco '(' The waves of the sea '), and represented the tide coming up on the reef. First of all the dancers formed a long line, then breaking the line they danced up ten or twelve at a time for a few steps, bending down their bodies and spreading out their hands, just as the little shoots from a wave run up the beach. Then wave after wave rolled in, those at the end running round but soon falling back again and the children forming the little wavelets. Then more and more waves, as the tide swung round to the shore side of the reef, and nothing but a small island of coral was left.

" The band kept up a sound like the roaring of

the surf, and as the tide rose the waves began to meet and battle over the little island, arms were thrown out in the air as they met, and the gauzy white streamers of the head-dresses shook like the spray. The idea of the dance could not have been more artistically carried out, and the people sitting round shouted with delight.

" Two other mékés followed, one an amusing pig-hunt. There must have been quite four thousand natives present; and as the missionary told me that none came from a distance of more than six miles, and there were very few women present in porportion to the number of men, the district must be still thickly peopled, although measles made fearful ravages here, this district alone losing eight thousand. One only hopes that no other imported disease will become epidemic. Every precaution is now being taken in the matter of quarantine, and doctors are making vaccinating tours through all the accessible districts."

The Missionaries, who have been so successful with the coast natives, have never been able to penetrate the central mountains of the big island, Viti Levu; and the hill-men, known as the Kai Tholo, are still heathen and cannibal. The only missionary who got among them was killed and eaten.

CHAPTER IX

NASOVA AND BAU

The Governor had appointed Mr Carew as commissioner of the mountain district of Viti Levu, and he had established a native constabulary camp at Nasathoco, high up the Singatoka river, in the hope of getting in touch with the Kai Tholo (or mountaineers) and preserving peace. Carew seemed to be getting on very well, and had persuaded a number of these hill-men to come down to the coast and meet the Governor. So we left Suva in H.M.S. *Nymphe*, and went to Navola on the south coast, where the meeting was to be held. This was the first I had seen of the Kai Tholo, wild-looking creatures, one or two of the younger ones stark naked and the others with the scantiest loin-cloth, but all with huge heads of hair. The Governor made a good speech to them, and they appeared to be impressed. In the evening they gave us a war dance. The cocoa-nut grove where they danced was illuminated with bonfires, and it was a most weird and striking scene.

At Serua we met one of the well-known old "beach combers" known as Cannibal Jack, who said his real name was Diaper, and the Governor and I had a long talk with him. His story is told

103

H

as " Jackson's Narrative " in Captain Erskine's book on the Pacific.[1] He said he had never really been a cannibal, but ended by saying that he thought Fiji was played out, and he meant to go to New Guinea to better himself.

We were back in Nasova in the middle of January, 1876, to the regular routine of business. I used to get away when possible for short expeditions at week-ends. I see in one letter, " Last Saturday I walked with Eyre over to Bureta on the other side of Ovalau, slept in the chief's house, and spent Sunday fishing the Bureta river, wading about four miles up to the village of Livone. The river looked lovely in the early morning. The Livone Valley itself is very beautiful, and the river in some places runs between big boulders with overhanging masses of vegetation and numbers of tree-ferns. We caught with a fly four or five dozen fish, from a few ounces to a pound in weight. Came back over the hills by another track on Sunday evening."

At other times we would go in a canoe inside the reef to the Island of Moturiki ; any change was good in this hot weather after a week's work.

About this time we had a great shock in the death of Mrs de Ricci, the wife of the Attorney General. They had arrived from England about the same time as we did. She was a pretty and agreeable woman only twenty-two years old.

Letter to my sister—

[1] *Journal of a Cruize among the Islands of the Western Pacific,* by John Erskine, Capt. R.N. John Murray, 1853.

" News from Samoa has just now reached us through Tonga, whither H.M.S. *Nymphe* had been sent on a cruise. It seems that Captain Stevens of the *Barracouta*, who has been backed up by the American Consul, has taken prisoner Colonel Steinberger (the American Filibuster who had set up a new Government in Samoa and given the natives much trouble), and has now got him safely locked up on board the *Barracouta*, and I suppose Captain Stevens is playing at being king of Samoa, an amusement that gallant captain will enjoy exceedingly. I don't suppose Stevens has the slightest right to imprison Steinberger, and some very amusing complications may arise. One good thing should come of it; it will wake up the people at home, and hurry on the preparation of the Governor's Commission as High Commissioner for the Western Pacific, which the lawyers are so slow in preparing. Report says that when Steinberger was arrested his *Commission from Washington* about which he boasted freely, and pretended it gave him great powers, proved to be two old passports pasted together."

I had written so much in my letter when a few days later I added, " On the 2nd April the barque *Etienne* arrived from Samoa with eight men from H.M.S. *Barracouta* on board, all wounded, in charge of a doctor; and two days later the *Barracouta* herself came in, and we heard the whole story. It seems to be something like this :

" ' After Steinberger had got himself appointed Premier of Samoa for life, and had been in the office some months, the King and some of the chiefs became tired of his behaviour, and the American Consul was equally anxious to get rid of him, and asked Stevens to take charge of Steinberger on board the *Barracouta*, as there was no American man-of-war in harbour, and he, the Consul, had no place in which to imprison him. This Stevens did, and then some of the followers of Steinberger (for many of the people thoroughly believed in him) said they would have nothing to do with a king who imprisoned their friend, and made up their minds to put someone else on the throne. In order to settle these difficulties there was to be a friendly meeting of chiefs. Captain Stevens went with the King to the meeting, accompanied by an armed guard of honour. When they landed, armed men were seen creeping through the bushes. The bluejackets were extended in skirmishing order, and somehow (it does not seem to be very clear how) shots were fired, first by the natives and then replied to by the sailors, and a regular skirmish began. It seems to have been a most casual affair, Captain Stevens carrying on a conversation with some of the chiefs all the time, and at last persuading them to stop their men firing. When once the fighting began the *Barracouta's* men seem to have behaved admirably. Three of them were killed and eight wounded, and I believe about nine Samoans fell.'

"Very soon after this happened, H.M.S. *Sapphire* arrived at Samoa to relieve the *Barracouta*, and I think Stevens was very glad to clear out. He came

here with two prisoners on board, Steinberger and
Coe, a former American Consul, and the day after
he arrived he managed to quarrel with Steinberger,
and washing his hands of him, landed him on the
beach. I think he was only too glad to get rid of
him, fearing the illegality of the arrest, and he
shunted his other prisoner in the same way. The
next day he sailed for Auckland, where he goes to
meet the Commodore, and I expect there will be
a 'jolly row'. Of course it is very difficult at present
to get at the truth, as everyone fears committing
himself, but the general impression seems to be
that Stevens interfered too much in Samoan affairs,
although he undoubtedly did good in ridding them
of Steinberger, and I don't see how he could help
staying at Samoa, when asked by the Consuls to
do so. In the barque that brought the wounded
men came Dr Steinberger, a brother of the Colonel.
Between the row in Samoa and an extra quantity
of gin, for which he has a liking, he seemed to have
got rather muddled, and when he arrived here was
afraid to come on shore lest he should be arrested !
At last he summoned up courage to come and see
the Governor. He was sober at the time, but looked
a very disreputable personage. He told the Governor
(with a very strong twang) that he 'had come out
to Samoa, expecting to find his brother Prime
Minister, and found instead that he was a prisoner
on board the *Barracouta*, but that if his brother
had committed any *indiscrepancies*, he supposed
it was right he should be there, and he should not

give him any support'. The officers of the *Barra-couta* seem to have liked the Colonel, and say he is a clever and amusing man, and a much better fellow in every way than the doctor. He messed with the ward-room officers, and I suppose they fed him well and gave him plenty of liquor, for he expressed his intention of letting the whole of America know the princely way he had been treated on a British man-of-war."

A long letter to my mother will go on with my story—

NASOVA,
FIJI,
April, 1876.

MY DEAR MOTHER,

"Mr Langham, the Missionary, is going for a three weeks' cruise amongst the Islands of his district; his wife goes with him, and during their absence they have lent the Governor their house at Bau. I go on ahead to-morrow in the gig. The Governor and Lady Gordon wait for the *Fitzroy* to take them; she is expected back this evening with the Mails from Kandavu. It is only twenty miles by water from Levuka to Bau. Baron Von Hügel goes with me.

BAU.

"We came down here very easily, under sail nearly all the way. As the water was too low for us to pass inside the reef round the Island of Moturiki, we had to row out through a very small passage to the open sea. The great big breakers were rolling

in ten yards either side of us, and when in the hollow
of the waves we could see the bright-coloured coral
not more than a couple of feet below the keel of
our boat. The swell was very heavy outside, but
luckily the wind was light; a row of a mile brought
us under the shelter of another reef, and we had
smooth sailing all the rest of the way. For some
miles round Bau, with the exception of one narrow
passage, the water is very shallow, but this gives
little trouble to the natives, whose canoes are of
very light draught, and who know every reef and
every bank by heart.

" The Missionary's house is right at the top of
the hill, and the view from it is charming. I don't
think any place has ever impressed upon me so
much as Bau how very small a town may be, and
yet be famous, or perhaps infamous. From reading
accounts of it I had begun to look on the story of
Bau and Fijian History much as one looks on the
story of Troy; it was shrouded in a sort of mysterious
past, and even meeting some of the actors in it
apart from the scene of action did not make the
story much more real to me. But looking over the
town from the hill where I sit writing this, seeing
the place where the cannibal ovens stood, counting
the death notches scored on the trees, and looking
on the very stone against which the victim's brains
were dashed out, whilst all round are the same
houses, the same canoes, the same people, makes it
very real indeed. The scene itself is actually before
you, and it wants very little change to turn that

large double canoe I can see gliding away towards
Ovalau, with fifty dark figures on its deck, to a
war party off on a marauding trip. The Island
itself does not measure much more than a quarter
of a mile in any direction, and the houses cannot
be counted by hundreds, but there is a dramatic
atmosphere about the place, and one cannot help
feeling that one is in a city and amongst a leading
people; and though no one can say that Bau is
beautiful, it is certainly beautifully picturesque.
On one side of the island, where there is but a strip
of land fifty or sixty yards broad between the steep
rocks and the shallow sea, stands the 'town' of
Thacombau the Vunivalu,[1] a cluster of some five
or six houses, his own of great size, and kitchen
and store-room nearly as big. There is a certain
air of quiet and grandeur about the place that I
can't describe. Nothing ever looks new about a
Fijian house, the walls and thatch so soon turn to
browns and greys of every shade. Clumps of hibiscus
with shining green leaves and bright scarlet flowers
grow half wild about the doors. Beyond the kitchen
is a large canoe shed, it holds but one double canoe,
but that canoe is over one hundred feet long and
would hold, they say, five hundred men. Imagine
what the size of the single mat sail must be to carry
such a ship along! The canoe is called the *Tavuki ni
Vanua*, 'the upsetting of the land', a traditional
and suggestive name that has belonged in turn to
all the biggest war canoes of the vunivalus of Bau.

---

[1] Vunivalu=Root of War.

The present one is being rebuilt, and I am looking forward to a promised sail in it when finished. The two hulls are old, but a new deck, mast, and deck house, etc., is being made for it. These huge hulls are made from hollowed trunks of trees, cleverly pieced together, every joint fastened with cocoa-nut sinnett; and not a single nail or metal bolt is used. In the old days they built their canoes with the aid of stone tools alone, now plane irons tied with sinnett into wooden handles, adze-like, have taken the place of the stone axes. It is a splendid sight to see a big canoe shooting along with a good breeze, the dark half-clothed figures on the deck forming the most picturesque groups. The chief stands in the stern to manage the huge steering oar, and the man with his hand on the sheet watches every movement of the sail and the thama [1] (for safety depends on his skill and quickness as much as on the helmsman himself) whilst a man forward, half-hidden in the hold, bails out the water that always foams over the pointed bow, and the crew grouped round the deck-house beat the lati and chant their quaint monotonous songs. Then, when a tack has to be made, all is bustle and excitement, for the foot of the great mat sail has to be dragged by sheer strength from one end of the canoe to the other—no easy work with any sea running. I am always hearing Fijians abused for the clumsiness of their canoes. I think most unfairly, for they are the only people I know of who, without the use of

---

[1] Thama=outrigger.

metal, and with no knowledge of building, have made boats safe to go to sea in, and able to beat to windward. But I am forgetting all about the Vunivalu's house. Lying on the mats and looking up into the roof, one's eyes lose themselves amongst the smoke-coloured rafters, and the platforms and store shelves where lie great bundles of sinnett and rolls of mats and canoe sails, in fact everything that means wealth to a Fijian. The first time I went into the house was in the evening. The old chief was sitting on his mat, his wife and daughter a little below him, not on the same mat, for that would have been a breach of good manners; and in a semi-circle in front of him, some lost to sight in the gloomy corners, sat groups of men and women. It was just meal-time, and the dinner began by a good-looking girl bringing some large green leaves with boiled yams in them, which she, kneeling down, spread out before the old chief; then, still bending down, she crawled back to her place near the door, for no one stands upright in so great a chief's presence. After the yams came fish, served in the same way, and when the chief had finished his food all the people clapped their hands. Then came tea and bread and butter, in which I joined, for having just dined I could not eat the yams that were offered to me. When the tea was over, there was more clapping of hands, and then all the rest fell to and dined off what was left. There seemed plenty for them all. They ate in silence, sitting in groups, men on one side of the door and women on the other. After dinner we had some conversation, but my interpreter, a Fijian, was so cowed in the presence of the great chief (generally he is the most free and easy, impudent scoundrel) that our talk was not very lively, and I was rather glad when the teacher came in, and we had family prayers, and the evening hymn sung with the usual Fijian drawl; and, whatever the tune, they always manage to end in a minor key. After prayers came *Yangona* (kava) and *Selukas* (cigarettes), and the old gentleman went off to bed. So we persuaded Andi Quila, his daughter, to take us to her own little house close by, and to send for one of her ladies to make another brew of yangona for us and roll selukas, and then chaffing and talking spent the rest of the evening, and I amused myself dressing up Andi Salotti, our yangona maker, in various bright-coloured shawls from Andi Quila's wardrobe, to suit my fancy. Andi Quila is such a fat, good-natured, handsome, cheery creature, and her children are charming.

" Yesterday we passed the morning wandering about the town, visiting different houses and looking at the big canoes. The first house we went into we found two women hard at work making earthen pots, and as they were still unbaked and soft I bought one, and set to work ornamenting my purchase with pictures of canoes, houses, palm-trees, etc., much to the amusement of my host and the two or three neighbours who had come in to see the strangers, whilst the Baron, sitting by the fire-place, distributed tobacco freely, and flirted with two rather pretty girls with white-limed hair. One of the men fed me at intervals with bits of the most delicious shaddock, from which he had taken off the rind and carefully removed all the pips. When I had finished my drawing, and Margerita (rather a dark one) had got all the tobacco out of the Baron's pockets, we wandered off again, leaving the pots to be baked and sent after us. Next we went into a house where the women were at work making *Masi*;[1] such a row they made, as they hammered out the bark on a resounding log of wood. Then we stopped to watch the men at work building houses and mending canoes, and finally we settled down at the house where Marioni, a pretty half-caste girl, lives with a very pleasant-looking old lady, her mother; and with Marioni and Andi Meri (who has the biggest black eyes in Bau) to prepare it for us we drank yangona, and drank too much of it. When first we asked Marioni to get some yangona for us, she, in fun, pretended there was none to be had, for which she got a snubbing from mamma, and was told to go and fetch a root directly and not behave 'vaka kai si' (like a common person) when a turaga (a chief) came for hospitality; in fact, the old lady did the honours properly, and was not a little distressed that we would sit by the fire-place and talk (I fear awful Fijian), and refused to sit on the mats on the dais and drink our yangona with proper solemnity. After this (perhaps the

---

[1] Masi=tappa, cloth made from the beaten-out bark of the paper mulberry.

114

effect of the yangona) I fell desperately in love with Marioni's sister, aged about six years, named Sariania. Such a picturesque little mite dressed in a little red sulu, with a pretty bead necklace and with her hair all combed up on end and white with lime, she helped in all the work of the house, and ran on messages with the air of doing most important business. I asked her to read to me, and she read away at the page I chanced to open the book, as fluently as possible.

" The Baron, who is well known here, has brought no end of presents, a smart sulu or pinafore for every pretty girl, and presents for some of the old women too. Luckily his affection for the young ladies is very evenly distributed, and they all seem to like him very much in return. Andi Quila, with whom he stayed some weeks at her house at Nasova, always calls him her son, and is really very fond of him indeed.

" In the afternoon we went to look at the Vunivalu's quarters by daylight, and Andi Quila showed us over the big kitchen, and then we walked back with the old chief, who was on his way to afternoon church. He was as pleased as possible at our praising his town.

" There is no end of church-going here. Every morning the lali (wooden drum) rings at sunrise for morning prayers; again about half-past five, after work is over, there is an afternoon service and a sermon; and, in the evening, family prayers in every house, and on Sunday they somehow manage to find time for another sermon and a Sunday School, at which even grown-up people attend. All this goes on just the same when there is no white parson in the place.

" I did not go down to Marioni's for yangona in the evening, but the Baron did, and from the want of sequence in his remarks on his return, and his anxiety to get to bed, I fancy those damsels must have brewed it strong.

24th April,

BAU.

" Here I have been for a week, and the Governor has not yet arrived. Every day last week we were on the look-out, expecting to see the *Fitzroy* appear in sight. Last Saturday, however, a canoe came from Levuka bringing me a letter from the Governor, saying that the *Fitzroy* had not yet returned with the mails from Kandavu (I suppose the San Francisco steamer is late, and she is waiting for her), that should she get back to Levuka before Wednesday he will start for Bau, but should he not arrive by that day I am to return to Nasova.

" I am sorry to say he also sends me news of slayings and burnings by the mountaineers of the Lingatoko district, of which I am most anxious to hear further particulars. What with hourly expecting the Governor to arrive, and the rainy weather, I have not left the island during the whole week, and am beginning to know which house in the town has the softest and cleanest mats. It may sound lazy, but it is a very pleasant way of spending

116

a hot day, lying on soft mats, being fanned and
having selukas rolled for you by the best-looking
girls in the place, in fact receiving all the attention
and hospitality a Fijian can offer. We have collected
the words of a good many native songs, and I have
assisted at the making of a good many ' pinafores ',
and they are much amused at my being able to sew
so well. When one speaks of pretty girls it is hardly
a fair term to use; they are most difficult people to
describe. Looking at them in church last Sunday,
I wondered how I could ever think or say that any
one of them was even decently good-looking, but
then they were all dressed up in ' pinafores ' of the
brightest colours and vilest taste, and had on great
stiff bunchy petticoats, an abomination encouraged
by the Missionaries. After church I delivered a
lecture on the subject, in my best Fijian, and actually
called Andi Meri a ' nigger ', though she has got
eyes as big as saucers, and when one sees her poling
a canoe dressed in a couple of yards of calico, or
in the dim light sitting cross-legged before the big
bowl, straining yangona, she looks magnificent. But
I think I reserve my greatest admiration for Andi
Litia. She is the daughter of Ratu Savenatha, one
of the highest chiefs in Fiji, and a brother of the
Vunivalu's. He died during the measles, and his
widow a few weeks ago married Ratu Izekeli, the
Roko Tui Ra (so hasty a marriage has shocked the
propriety of the Bau ladies most dreadfully); so
Litia is left to herself at the age of seventeen.
She is a great lady, one of the best born in the

land. She has her house at Bau, and numbers of attendants and followers, to whom she is rather imperious; altogether for a Fijian she is I suppose very well off. She is the quaintest little thing you ever saw, very well made, with the prettiest little feet and hands; her eyes are a trifle oblique, but she has the most charming little neck, of which I think she is fully aware, for no one has such pretty bead necklaces. She is full of fun, but perfectly lady-like in her manner, and does the honours of her house gracefully and without the least sign of shyness. One hardly expects amongst a semi-civilized people to find a young girl holding such a position, but at Bau the women have always been well treated, and often exercise great influence. At the present time Andi Quila is virtually Roko Tui of a large province, and has been so since the death of her husband, but she cannot take the title, and receives her pay from Government in the form of a pension and not as a salary.

" As there was a very low tide this morning all the young ladies of the place were out fishing, about fifty of them, with Andi Quila as leader; they wade and swim about from reef to reef, and forming large circles gradually close in until, with a great deal of shouting and splashing, they are close enough together to make a complete ring with the oblong nets they carry in their hands. They were away all day, and this evening we had presents of fish from Andi Quila, Andi Litia and Andi Meri, so we are well off for supper. Our provisions, I must tell you, have been running very short, but we happily found a cupboard in Mr Langham's house filled with good things, and since this grand discovery we have fared sumptuously. The Baron, who has regular mat fever, has been miserable all day, for, the women all being away fishing, he could get no one to roll selukas or make yangona for him.

"I have been writing a good deal about the ladies because it is the first time I have really seen much of them in their own houses. The men I have told you about often before. Many of the Bau men are so handsome and well made that I think they would look well anywhere (provided of course, they are not dressed up in bright blue velvet coats and knickerbockers and tall white hats, the costume in which the late Prime Minister, Mr Woods, insisted on the Vunivalu appearing in public). The women, on the other hand, owe much more of their attraction and picturesqueness to their surroundings, and lose half their charm when taken away from their own houses.

"On Tuesday we rowed over to the mainland, and then walked over to pay a visit to Mr Witherow, a planter on the Rewa. It was a very pretty walk of about six miles, but the path was a good deal flooded from the late rains, sometimes waist-high; this path strikes the river about twenty miles from its mouth. The Witherows were delighted to see the Baron, who had stayed with them for some time on one of his trips. They are a very good sort of people, though, like all Fijian planters, miserably poor. Their house is well placed, overlooking the river, and the garden is the best I have yet seen. Andi Quila's big house is just on the opposite side of the river at Navuso. I was rather sorry not to go over and have a look at it, but all the canoes were out, and Mr Witherow was painting his boat, so there was nothing to take us across.

"It was nearly dark when we got to the end of our walk homewards, and it was no easy work crossing a creek about two hundreds yards wide on a bridge of single logs supported on crossed sticks. As we had our thick boots on it was impossible to walk over it, and my feet were so tender from the effects of walking on a coral reef that I dare not take my boots off. The Baron was in much the same condition, so we scrambled along as best we could, but by the time we got to the middle the Baron, who was going first, was in such fits of laughter that it was impossible to get him along, and had not two natives come to our rescue with long bamboos I believe we should have been there all night. At the village on the banks of the creek we found waiting for us the canoe we had ordered, and we paddled back to Bau.

"I was quite sorry when Wednesday passed and the Governor did not appear. We drank many farewell bowls of yangona that evening, and about half past six the next morning started in the gig for Levuka. There was not a breath of wind, and we had a weary pull over to the little island of

Leluvia, the island where in old times Thacombau used to send all married couples who could not agree, to stay there until they were good friends again. There we waited for the men to have their breakfast, whilst I had a bathe. Then we pulled on inside the reef, round the end of Moturiki. The glare from the shallow water and the white sandy bottom was terrible, and the men, who were suffering from the effects of ten days' idleness with unlimited food, tobacco and yangona, were thoroughly beat. It was all I could do to persuade them to pull on over the shallows before the tide fell too low; we did ground once, but got off again. At last we saw blue water close ahead of us, and then we all jumped overboard and sat in the water to cool ourselves, until someone saw a shark, when we all scrambled back into the boat again as fast as we could. An hour's row brought us opposite one of the villages on the coast of Ovalau, where we landed and had our lunch and an hour's sleep, then pulled on to Nasova and arrived there about four o'clock. The Governor was standing to meet me at the end of the pier, with the news that the *Fitzroy* had just come in, and that they were all off to Bau to-morrow, so our journey back was useless, but there had been no means of stopping us.

"I hurried off to town before the stores were closed to buy some presents to take back with me, and in the evening heard all the news about the Singatoka rising, which I must tell you later on.

"The next morning we started for Bau. We

were a large party of ourselves, and Andi Alisi, the wife of Ratu Vuki the Roko Tui Ba, her brother Joni Tholata, and some of her attendants came with us. Alisi had come up with her husband on a visit to Levuka and Bau, but when the news of the Singatoka troubles arrived, the Governor sent Ratu Vuki off in the *Star of the South* back to his own province, which is next to the disturbed district, and Andi Alisi is left to follow with her attendants in the canoes that have brought them, which are now lying at Bau.

" The Missionary's house would not hold nearly all our party ; so some of us took up our quarters at the Vunivalu's, and some at the Native ' Stranger's house ', where we were very comfortable.

" I told you in another letter how I had to return to Levuka again to make arrangements for starting with the Governor for the North West Coast of Viti Levu. I managed, however, to get back to Bau in time for the great méké on Tuesday. Unluckily it was a bad day, and was showery nearly all the afternoon. Only two days' notice had been given, yet about a thousand people came over from the mainland, and some of the mékés were excellent. One, danced by men from the Bigland, was particularly curious. It was an old heathen méké, and was supposed to represent the actions and powers of a certain god. The men dancing in it were all dressed nearly alike, in likus and garlands of green leaves. I could not understand a word of the song, and even Mr Wilkinson could only catch a word now and then. The movements of the dance were curious but very graceful, and it ended by the god (represented by *two* men who sat on the ground with their backs towards us) asking for food. The dancers moved up in two lines from opposite sides, and as each man passed the god he pretended to place some food before him. But the god was very hungry, and as soon as one man had brought him food, he beckoned to the next man to come on, waving his hands up to his mouth to show that he wanted more. The men came quicker and quicker, and the god's four hands kept beckoning and waving them on, until the men came racing up to him. At last he had eaten until he could eat no more, and then he (the two men) fell flat on his back with his hands stretched out behind him.

" But the event of the day was a Tongan méké danced by the ladies of Bau led by Andi Quila. I had seen and heard a great deal about the making of the dresses for this dance, and had myself brought back from Levuka a lot of material as presents for my friends. The colours were very carefully chosen, and with Lady Gordon's help I had sketched out several costumes which we prided ourselves were in very good taste. But what was my horror as the women filed past, to see that they had mixed and exchanged with one another all the things I had given them, and made their dresses up to suit their own fancy. I must say that though individually they might have been dressed in better taste, the general effect of the mass of colours was good. The méké was pretty but rather monotonous. Each woman carried a little paddle in her hand, and I believe the song had something to do with canoeing, but what it was I could not find out. The band consisted of Old Joeli, the chief native minister (missionary) at Bau, who is a Tongan, and two assistants, who played or rather beat time on a very noisy log of wood, and sang the beginning of every line of the song, which was taken up a third lower by the dancers. It was very different from any Fijian méké I have seen, and was, I believe, first brought here for the opening of the Missionary College at Navuloa, when a number of Tongan ladies were invited and entertained at Bau for several months, so that the Fijians might learn to dance it properly."

CHAPTER X

MOUNTAIN WAR

" I must interrupt this letter to say that news had reached us that the Kai Tholo had made a descent on their hereditary enemies the coast natives, and there had been burnings and slayings, so that it was evident we were in for a little war. Colonel Pratt, in command of the small body of R.E.'s, told the Governor that he would not move a man until he had received reinforcements from Australia or the Cape. Now as rapid action was necessary, and it was very desirable to avoid a war of races, the Governor took the bold stroke of putting the disturbed districts outside the jurisdiction of the Supreme Court and treating the whole matter as one to be left to the native police under the command of Captain Knollys.

" We should all of us have liked to stay longer at Bau, but it was important that the Governor should go off to the disturbed districts as soon as possible. So on Wednesday morning we all went back to Levuka in the *Fitzroy*.

" Our few hours at Nasova were very busy ones, for we were to start again in the *Fitzroy* for the north west coast of Viti Levu early the next morning.

125

There was a fortnight's provisions to be got on board, a police guard to be armed and got ready, and despatches to be written for the English mail, which would have left before our return. Mr Wilkinson, the chief interpreter, was to come with us. The Baron, who stayed at Nasova with Lady Gordon and the children, gave me all the hints he could about the places worth visiting, and the country and villages we were likely to pass through, for he had spent some time on the north west coast during his wanderings about Viti Levu.

"With all our hurrying it was ten o'clock before we started, and though we had a fair wind down the coast, the sun had set some time before we dropped anchor in Raki Raki Bay, opposite to Na Vatu, and it was too late to land and sleep on shore as we had intended. As it was but a short day's journey to Ba we determined to land the next morning at Na Vatu, a large pile or rock rising boldly fro m the water's edge, and have a look at the town before the *Fitzroy* got under way.

"We set off in one of the ship's boats before sunrise. In the uncertain light it was difficult to judge our distance from the shore, and in our tub of a boat it proved a much longer pull than I expected; it was so late when we landed that there was only time to visit hastily the village at the foot of the rock, have a bathe, and get back to the steamer as quickly as possible. I was sorry not to see more of the place, for its position is curious. A range of bare-looking mountains follows the line of the bay some distance inland, bare, that is, of trees, but grass-covered nearly to their rocky summits. A plain lies between these mountains and the sea, broken only where Na Vatu rises abruptly at the water's edge. Though not many hundred feet high, the rock is imposing and picturesque, both from its position and its shape. It held a high place in the mythological stories of Fiji, as one of the 'jumping-off places' into the world of spirits. There are now three villages on the rock, the one we visited, at the bottom, one halfway up on the land side, and one perched almost on the top.

"On our way to Ba we met Ratu Vuki's three canoes lying in a dead calm. They had left Bau for Ba the day we left for Ovalau, hoping to get home in time to receive us. The country we were passing was barer of trees and less tropical-looking at every point we turned, and by the time we arrived off the Ba river it was easier to imagine oneself looking on the Western Highlands of Scotland than the mountains of an island in the South Seas.

"We had to anchor some distance from the land, for, as is the case with all Fiji rivers, the passage to the river's mouth is a winding and difficult one. We started in the gig to row up to Sagunu, the home of the Roko. The river is a fine broad stream, but the banks are low, and fringed with mangroves for the first mile or so. Above the mangrove forest the land seemed good, and we passed several large food plantations and some fine old groves of ivi trees. About an hour and a half's row brought us to the town, which is so well hidden in a dense grove of ivi and breadfruit trees that one might easily pass up the river without knowing of its existence. But once inside the grove there seem to be numberless houses dotted about amongst the trees, and in some places regular little streets of them. The style of building here was quite new to me. The posts that support the walls of the houses are set square, and one large central post supports the somewhat dome-like roof of thatch and bamboo rafters. The walls too are thatched with grass, and from the outside it is hard to say where the walls end and the roof begins. Each house stands on a built-up mound, about four feet above the ground level on account of the floods. But few have more than one door, and that seems usually closed; windows there are none. A good path leads up to the *rara*, where the Roko's house stands. The house is a new one, in shape the same as those of the east coast, but with a Tongan roof, stronger perhaps, but not so pleasing in arrangement as a Fijian roof. The house is divided into compartments by two well-made reed partitions, and is very comfortable, though the European writing-table, chest of drawers, etc., looked rather odd and out of place. But Ratu Vuki is a good man of business; and the pigeon-holes of his bureau are full of papers, and he was able to put his hand directly on one that was wanted, an improvement on the usual Fijian fashion of hiding away all letters and papers under the mats.

"In one of the scrimmages on the Singatoka

river three mountaineers had been taken prisoners. The people of Nandronga (where they had first been taken to) were able to get but very little information out of them as to the state of affairs in their towns, and the reasons for the beginning of the present trouble, so had handed them over to Ratu Vuki, in the hope that when right away from their own people something might be got out of them. The Governor said he would like to see them. Whilst the prisoners were being sent for, we went to have a swim in the river, and on our return found them in the house—three old men, with rather dirty sulus [1] round them, which they seemed anxious to be rid of! The Governor had a long conversation with them, the interpretation of which was rather amusing, each sentence going through a sort of process of filtration. The mountain talk, although the same language, is so distinct a dialect that coast natives understand very little of it. All the Governor said had to be turned by Mr Wilkinson into the Bau language, then from him it went, with the help of the Roko, to a Nandi man, who turned it into the mountain dialect for the prisoners, who were all old and rather deaf, and two out of the three very stupid. As you may imagine, the conversation was not very rapid ; however, a little more was got out of them than was known before.

" Andi Alisi arrived during the night, and when I met her the next morning she seemed still terribly put out at not having arrived here in time to receive

[1] Loin-cloths.

the Governor. About breakfast-time the village people came to the Roko's house with presents of food for the Governor. Every house in the village must have brought its contribution, and there was quite a crowd outside waiting to present their offerings. Three or four women at a time came into the house and placed their present of boiled yams or taro, served up in banana leaves (with sometimes the addition of a boiled chicken, were the giver rich enough) in front of the Governor. As soon as the present was accepted, the women went out and another party came in; there seemed to be no end to them, and the slaughter amongst the chickens must have been terrible. I am glad to say one is not expected to eat all that is given, as I have no doubt some ten boiled chickens and thirty or forty pounds of yams might have fallen to my share.

"The Governor would, of course, have stopped all this food being cooked had he known of it in time, but Ratu Vuki had said nothing about it, and, as he told us afterwards, he found himself in rather a difficult position. He knew the Governor's dislike to accepting such presents, and on the other hand (although its ruler), not being a native of the place himself, he did not like to check the people in their own mode of showing respect to the Governor, so he thought it best to hold his tongue. But he was evidently very well pleased at the way in which the people had come forward with—in a Fijian's eyes—so handsome a present. The food was left with the Roko, and I suppose by him distributed amongst the people again, but the waste on these occasions is very great, and in the old days was something dreadful, as a chief judged of his reception by the amount of food presented to him; and although there might be plenty in the district at the time, the inroads made on the stores often caused famine before the crop season came round again. Luckily this custom is gradually giving way, and visitors are fed for a day by each house in turn during their stay in a village.

"After breakfast the Roko took us for a walk round his town, which is even larger than I at first thought, and the food plantations all round it seem to be in capital order. Some few of the houses have tops to their doorways unlike any I have seen before, and rather pretty.

"About twelve o'clock we started in the gig for the *Fitzroy*, and a good breeze took us quickly down the river and out to the vessel. It was late when we arrived at Nandi, so we slept on board that night and landed next morning at the town of Ne Rewa, about a mile up the Nandi river, taking up our quarters at the house of Na Vula (the moon), the Buli [1] of the district, who of course cleared out for us. The house was quite a new one, and but for the mosquitoes and rats, both a good deal too numerous, we were very comfortable. We had brought no end of provisions with us, and these we housed in the Government store, which has been set up here under the charge of a white man, since

[1] Administrative chief.

131

the beginning of the troubles in the mountains.

" The town is newly built, having been moved from its old site up the river after the panic caused by the measles, and it is certainly a change for the worse. The mangrove-fringed river, with great stretches of muddy sand left bare at low tide, the groves of tall cocoa-nut trees, and the square grass-thatched houses standing on dry sandy ground, came much nearer to my idea of an African village and its surroundings than a Fijian town, and I am glad there are not many more like it. The weather was beautifully fine and cool, and the moonlight nights were lovely. Every night during the five days we were at Na Rewa, the mats were spread outside the house, and the natives sat in a great semi-circle in front of us, and chanted their drinking songs whilst the yangona was being strained.

" On his arrival at Na Rewa the Governor had sent up letters to Captain Knollys to arrange a meeting with him at the village of Wai Wai half-way between Na Rewa and Nasauthoko, and had suggested that if the risk were not great, he should like to go on to Nasauthoko itself. Mr Carew, the Commissioner, whom we had met at Na Rewa, and who had returned to Levuka the next day in the *Fitzroy*, quite approved of this arrangement. We spent the days we had to wait for an answer from Knollys in walking about the country and visiting the white settlers. At the back of Na Rewa is a plain of considerable extent, and on it, chiefly near the banks of the river, are six or seven estates of

white settlers, known generically as ' Nandi Planters '.
They seem to be good friends with one another,
and their hatred and opposition to the old Government was so strong as nearly to lead to a Civil War.
I found them a much better lot of fellows than
I expected, but all terribly hard up. Like most of
the Fiji planters, they had come here at the time of
the cotton mania, bought land, hired Polynesian
labourers and had one good crop and promise of
rapid wealth. Then came the fall in prices, and
five or six bad years had swallowed up all profit,
exhausted their capital, and left them as we find
them now, burdened with debt, living from hand
to mouth, sending perhaps a few bags of maize to
the Australian or New Zealand market, but sometimes
only growing enough food to feed the labourers, whom
they are not able to employ profitably, yet can't
afford to send back to their own islands ; waiting
anxiously for the passing of a bankruptcy law to
free them from their debts, and the Government's
approval of their land-titles, and with the small
amount of money thus raised try their luck again
here, or clear out of the country altogether.

" The Nandi Planters are industrious and hard-
working men, and certainly deserve a better fate.
They say that since the failure of cotton they can
find nothing that they can grow with any certainty
of profit ; even maize has fallen so low in price that
they are growing less and less of it every year. Yet
the Nandi Plain is certainly very fertile ; there is
no expense for clearing, and ploughs are in use in

133

every estate. A good road to the bay, and a little fresh capital, will no doubt bring prosperity to the district, but I doubt if the present planters will be able to hold out long enough to reap the benefits of a change, should it come.

"On Wednesday morning came a letter from Knollys saying that he would be at Wai Wai to meet us early on Friday morning. I spent the day making preparations for our start on the morrow. First of all the arms of our Guard had to be looked to, and a very poor lot they proved. Two Terry breach-loaders, four muzzle-loading Enfields, and the rest old German smooth-bore muskets in various stages of decay. To find out if they were any use at all I had a blank cartridge fired out of each (I took care not to fire them myself); one half of them refused to go off the first time, but with a good deal of coaxing the useless ones were at last reduced to three or four, and these we managed to replace by a few that had been left in the Government store. The next difficulty was to provide something for the men to carry their ammunition in, as sulus have no pockets, and only half the men had pouches or belts, so we set to work making belts and pouches out of bits of canvas from despatch bags, sewn together with some red tape that I had in my des-patch box, for string we had none. In the afternoon I went with the Governor and Mr Wilkinson to inspect the schoolchildren. About one hundred and fifty of them were waiting for us in the church, and after the usual reading and writing had been gone through, all the children turned out into the rara for a méké, and through Mr Wilkinson and the native parson I managed to make out some thing of the meaning of the song. It was a lesson in natural history that had certainly never been taught them by a white missionary. All the children were seated on the ground, and in a rhythmic chant they told about all the birds and insects, imitating their cries and giving descriptions of their habits, which were scarcely scientifically correct. When they came to the mosquito they began to hum and buzz and slap their arms and legs as if they had just felt a mosquito in the act of biting them. All this was part of the song and done in the most perfect time; then, as if driven half wild with the irritation, they shouted and threw their arms about, and then suddenly stopped, exhausted, saying that there was nothing for it but to bear the pain patiently, and when the mosquitoes sung songs in their ears to cry, 'Vinaka', 'Vinaka' in applause. When they came to man, they told us that when a man died all the animals were pleased, but the ants rejoiced most of all, for they dig down through the earth where his body lies buried, and carry off his teeth, for a man's teeth are the ants 'tambuas' (whales' teeth ornaments). The mosquito alone is sorry, and hovers about humming a mournful song. 'What good', says he, 'is a man to me when he is dead? I can neither drink his blood nor sing songs into his ears.'

CHAPTER XI

VITI LEVU

"At waking next morning we were not a little surprised to hear that Arthur Gordon and his interpreter had arrived during the night. On receiving a letter the Governor had sent them from Na Rewa—they had hurried over to see him before he started for Nasauthoko—walking all the way from Nandronga in two days. They were, of course, very tired, and, as we had not much time to spare to talk to them, it was arranged that they should follow us to Nasauthoko as soon as they had recovered from the effects of their hard walk. It was no easy work starting carriers, but at last we got off about seven o'clock, trusting to Gordon to send on anything we might have left behind us. Old Na Vula, the Buli, came with us, bringing about twenty armed followers with him.

"It was a long and rather weary trudge over the plain. We found it impossible to keep the carriers in front of us; they straggled all over the place, and every now and then we had to wait for them to come up. About midday we stopped about an hour at the river to bathe and have lunch. Here old Na Vula gave in and said he could go no further, his feet were so bad. The Governor told him he might go back if he liked, but refused to let his men go back with him, as he might have need of them.

"After crossing the river we left the plain; there were two or three low ridges in front of us, and then, standing out on the shoulder of the hill, overhung by a big black rock, we could see the village of Vatutoko. It was a good long climb up to the village, and we had to wait some time when we got there for the carriers to catch us up. The village was but a collection of a few tumble-down huts. It has not been properly rebuilt since it was burnt down by the Kai Tholo a few years ago. Some hundred feet below us, nestled in a hollow on the bank of the stream we had crossed, we could see the pretty little village of Koro Koula (Red Town), named, I suppose, from the bare patch of red earth by it. The village itself is built on a patch of white sand, and looked a picture of neatness, with a green hedge all round it, and the houses all built in regular order—a rare thing in a Fijian town! The view from our resting-place was very extensive, taking in the whole plain of Nandi and the Bololo and Yasava Islands dotted over the sea in the distance. They fetched us some water from the villages; it was deliciously cool, and, as is the fashion in this part of the country, it was brought to us in a bamboo about eight feet long—not an easy thing to drink out of if one has no cup. Then, as most of our carriers had come up and there was yet two hours' daylight, we agreed to push on to Wai Wai, a fortified town, and the usual resting-place between Nandi and Nasauthoko.

"Our path lay along the main ridge nearly the whole distance. The slopes of the hills on either side of us were broken up into thousands of little grass-covered hillocks and dells, as if to see how much surface there could be in a given space. There was not much wood except on the higher hill-tops, and altogether the country gave one the idea (which does not prove true) of the approach to a great mountain range.

"The evening closed in grey and dull, and, as we came close to Wai Wai, the rain that had all day been hanging about the hill-tops came down in heavy showers. We found only part of the town fortified, that is, enclosed in a rotten-looking bamboo fence, and surrounded by a fighting ditch much overgrown. The best-looking house was outside the fence, but, as we were now fairly in the enemy's country, it was only prudent to take up our quarters inside, with all our guard, in case of an attack. As soon as we got our traps in the shelter of a house I started off with the Governor to examine the approaches to the town, and post the sentries. It was not a pleasant night to keep guard, as the rain was still falling, and as we had risen 1,750 feet (by my barometer) we felt the cold keenly. Out of our force of twenty-six 'Sotias'[1] we could not afford more than five sentries, three outside and two inside the fence, and left the hills to be guarded by the 'Taukais'

[1] Armed police.

138

(native proprietors). Who should I see on coming back to the village but old Na Vula, who had followed us up in spite of his bad feet. The chief of the town, a bright-looking fellow, presented his root of yangona, someone slew a chicken, and with the teacher and Na Vula as guests we had our dinner; then, as mine was the middle watch, I turned in for the night.

NASAUTHOKO,
Saturday.

"Soon after I turned out yesterday morning Knollys arrived with thirty of his own men and fifty allies, under the command of Neamani, a friendly chief. A very barbaric-looking force they were— faces painted black and red, streamers, sashes and turbans of white or smoke-browned masi, white or scarlet sulus, or long black bead-strung likus, and big fighting fans in the hands of every chief. Each dress seemed more fantastic than the last one I had looked at, and many of my old acquaintances were so disguised by their war-paint that I could not recognize them. The European guns and cross-belts seemed somehow to add to their fierce barbaric appearance.

"After breakfast, as Knollys had no objection to the plan, we packed up our traps and started for Nasauthoko. The road passed through broken uplands, slightly timbered and with but a poor-looking soil. Nothing could have looked more picturesque than our guard, winding along the track in single file, with a young chief running ahead, quivering his big war fan. The man just in front of me for the first few miles, though by no means the most fantastically dressed, is a fair specimen to describe. He was a fine tall fellow with a shining brown skin; his face was blackened all over, and his head done up in folds of brown gauze-like masi, arranged somewhat in the shape of a Parsee's hat ; round his neck was a piece of red cloth, and fastened to it behind were two long folds of brown masi, which hung down below his waist, or streamed out in the wind. A black leather cross-belt and pouch were the only parts of his dress that could be called uniform. Round his waist he wore a sash of scarlet cloth, and a huge black water-weed liku hung in strings to his knees; his legs were gartered with fringed rolls of the same weed strung with many coloured beads.

"After the first four miles the road passed through patches of wood, and though fair for a mountain path, it was not the very best walking. But the air was delicious and the sun not a bit too hot. Soon we got amongst the big dakua pines— fine trees with straight round trunks forty or fifty feet without a branch. A turn in the road brought us in sight of the two round-fenced towns of Nasauthoko in the plain, some two thousand feet below us. The country now opened a good deal, for we had passed the coast range of hills, and though we had to go through several miles of dense forest, at nearly every open space we came to during the rest of our walk we had extensive views over the hills and valleys for many miles around. We passed two fine cataracts, but not close enough to see them well, and the natives pointed out several strongholds of the 'Devils', places we already knew well by name and reputation.

"I made the highest point we mounted 2,300 above the sea, and the descent to Nasauthoko (which stands only about three hundred feet above sea-level) was rather trying to my foot, which had been painful ever since we started from Nandi. The general character of the country is hilly rather than mountainous, varied with rock, forest and grass. It is well watered, and there are small fertile-looking grass plains in the river bottoms.

"Although I kept a sharp look-out to mark the character of the country we were passing through, it was hard to take one's eyes off the movements of our escort. Every turn in the track, the view from every hill, showed them to fresh advantage; climbing up a bare hillside with their masi streamers flying in the wind, or grouping themselves on hill-tops to rest after an ascent, they seemed to form picture after picture, perhaps the most striking of all when, through a tunnel of trees, they scrambled down a steep hillside, and were gradually lost to sight in the dark wood at the bottom. Every moment one saw a fresh headdress or a new style of ornament; one man had his head covered with brown masi bound on with a fringe of white, and a long queue of brown hanging behind, tied up like a bag wig. Another man had on what looked like a very tall stiff white nightcap. A third had his masi arranged with a sort of plume in front. In fact, there were not two of them alike.

"Nasauthoko is a great place for making white masi, and the 'Sotias' amuse themselves in camp by smoking it to a brown colour, or dyeing it yellow with turmeric.

"At last, crossing a small river, we came to the camp itself. Outside the fence the sotias, with Ratu Tevita at their head, were drawn up as a guard of honour. All were as smartly dressed as those who were with us. We first passed through a low guarded bamboo gateway, and then along a narrow path, between two fences of bamboo, to the guard-house, which is most picturesquely perched over the second gateway. The last and strongest fighting fence is built on the top of a bank of earth, thrown up in digging the ditch outside. The bank itself is loop-holed, and I think the Kai Tholo would have had work to break their way in. The camp consists of seven or eight hastily built houses, the one we are put up in is much like the house we have been living in at Nandi. We were glad to hear that Koli Koli, the chief from Beimana, whom the Governor was most anxious to see, was in camp.

"After dinner Neamani brought in the Taukais of the native town of Nasauthoko, who came to present their root of yangona, and with them came Koli Koli and his two followers. The Governor made the Taukais a short speech, thanking them for their loyalty, etc. This was translated into Fijian by Mr Wilkinson, and from him into the mountain

dialect by Neamani, who proved an excellent speaker.
Then the Governor presented them with tambuas
(whale's teeth), which they received with many deep-
drawn breaths, something between a sigh and a
grunt. After drinking yangona all round, Ratu
Tevita asked whether we would have ' lotu ' (evening
prayer) as usual. I was afraid, when the Governor
said ' Yes ', that our friend the Nandi parson,
who was in the house, and who is always a trifle
long-winded, might think it too good a chance to
be lost of giving good advice in his prayers to his
mountain and heathen hearers ; but as far as I
could understand him (and I don't suppose the
mountaineers understood much more than I did)
his prayers were very moderate and sensible. After
prayers the Nasauthoko people went off, and the
Governor had a long talk with the Koli Koli, inter-
preted as before, but Tevita would keep putting in
his oar, and ' assisting ' in the interpretation, and
between the three of them poor Koli Koli got such
a lecturing that I hardly thought he would have
the pluck to reply. Much to my surprise he began
a long story, and told us all he knew about the history
of the rising, most carefully. How that after a
meeting at Na Vola he had called a meeting of the
Nanganga people and all the other towns in his
neighbourhood, and asked them to join him in
being of good mind towards the Matanitu (Government), for the Matanitu wished for peace and plenty,
and that was more to his mind than war and famine.
How first of all some were of his opinion, but finally

the advice of the younger men prevailed, and he was left alone to return to his own home. Then some of the men of his own town deserted him, and turned against him, and, as he afterwards heard, advised his neighbours, now his enemies, to attack him. Fearing an attack the people still faithful to him took it in turns to keep watch at night. One night his younger brother, the ' Turanga ni lewa ' (law chief) woke him up to tell him that he could not sleep for ' Sese ' (a pain in the big toe), and that it was clear the enemy must be coming. They had not received any warning of the movements of Trevoro (devils), but (on the strength of the Sese) they both got up and watched, and presently saw four men entering the town. He, Koli Koli, called out asking who they were, and they replied they were Wai Levu people come to kill him and his family. He told them to go away, remembering that Mr Carew had told him never to begin a fight; but the Turanga ni lewa, fearing that too many men would enter the town and overpower them, fired, and all the rest followed his lead. In the fighting that followed they saw two of the enemy fall dead and one wounded, but as the moon was setting he would not let his people follow the enemy out of the town, fearing an ambush, but the enemy troubled them no more that night. One dead body they secured, and brought it the next evening to Nasauthoko to show to the ' Turanga ni Matanitu ' as a proof of their loyalty."

The description of the bringing of the body I take from one of Knollys' letters to the Governor—

"I hope I have not been aiding and abetting heathen rites, but as the people who brought the dead man here from Beimana made a point of my seeing the body, I went to the village to do so. It was a curious sight by torchlight to see the poor man slung on a bamboo with about sixty of the wildest people I ever saw dancing round it, and making speeches. They wound up by a half-joking request to be allowed to eat him, and half a hint would have made them do so. However, I ordered him to be buried at once, as he had been kept quite long enough."

"When Koli Koli had finished his story, the Governor asked him if he could give him any help. He shook his head and seemed suspicious and un-easy at the thought of any 'sotias' coming to strengthen his town, saying they were foreigners, and bearing in mind, I think, the stories and traditions of the old mountain warfare, not always to the credit of the more civilized part of the community. How-ever, he went away, I think, quite contented, with the Governor's approval of his plan of sending for some of his people from outlying villages to come and strengthen Beimana, and a promise of help from Nasauthoko whenever he should send for it.

"Next morning we climbed to the top of a neighbouring hill to get a view over the country, and take some compass bearings in order to sketch out a rough map. When we came back to the camp all the sotias were paraded, and the Governor made

145

a speech to them, and shook hands with and thanked the native officers, and then started off for Wai Wai with Knollys and an escort. As my foot was still painful, and Gordon was at Nandi to do any writing work, it was arranged that I should stop and rest for a day or two at Nasauthoko. Mr Wilkinson also remained, Dr MacGregor returning with the Governor.

"Knollys slept the night at Wai Wai, and did not get back to camp until Sunday morning. The Governor had told him on parting that as soon as he got to Na Rewa, he would send back a messenger to tell him what his next movements were to be, and most likely would send Gordon up to Nasauthoko to have a talk over their plans.

"On Tuesday morning no messenger had arrived, and as the camp was running very short of food, Knollys thought it time to make a raid on the enemy's plantations. He did not like to leave the camp himself, expecting that Gordon might arrive, so sent sixty of his police under Tevita and about the same number of Taukais under Neamani. It was such a lovely morning and my foot was so much better that I could not resist the temptation to go with them. Our hunting grounds were to be the river flats of the Singatoka near Vatu Mali, one of the enemy's towns burnt a few weeks since. It promised to be a hot day, but the air was beautifully clear, and right to the far distance the mountain tops stood out clear and sharp. Tevita and Neamani seemed determined to take good care of me; they impressed the parson (who was of course armed himself) into my service to carry my rifle and ammunition, and one or other of them insisted on carrying me over the many brooks and rivulets we passed. For the first two or three miles our way lay through small patches of forest, then the country opened again and we came to the hill where the police had been stopped on their first march into the interior. Neamani told me the whole story as we neared the spot, pointing out where the 'tevoro' were posted, where Olive sat, etc., etc. I could understand but a small part of what he said, but Neamani is a born story-teller, and his gestures and actions made the story intelligible. The view from the top of the hill was lovely. Here Tevita called a halt, and whilst he, Neamani, and I rested on one little hillock, the men grouped themselves on a hill facing us about twenty yards distant, and on the crescent-shaped ridge between. Then Tevita rose and made a long speech, urging them to act like brave men, and working on their war-like feelings. As he warmed to his work, he called out in turn to the men of each district, asking, 'Could they fight? What deed would they have to boast of when the war was over?' Then, as the name of the land was called out, the sotias from that place rushed out like wild men from the crowd, dancing frantically in front of us, and shaking their guns in our faces, made their boast of what they would do, and they were far from modest in speaking of their own prowess. Any boast more venturesome than another was hailed with shouts of 'Vinaka Vinaka tangane'. Then they fell back among their comrades, and their excitement seemed to die away as rapidly as it rose.

"When the men from each district had made their 'Bole' (boast), Tevita wound up his oration with a warning that I had hardly expected from him, telling them that they must bear in mind that they were no longer making war Vaka Viti, but Vaka Piritania (British fashion); that should any fighting occur that day they were not to rush forward to club fallen men for the honour of securing the bodies, and above all they were to spare and protect women and children.

"The speech over, we tramped another mile or so to the top of another hill, where we halted again. This time it was the parson's turn, and laying his rifle on the ground before him, he gave out the morning prayers.

"We were now on the low hills just above the river flats, and we could see the banana leaves and cane-tops down by the water's edge. After prayers half our company opened out into a sort of loose skirmishing order and all made their way through the long grass down the hillside, the young chiefs running up and down in front of the line, flourishing their fans and beating the grass with them, as though they expected to find an enemy under every blade. It was a very pretty sight to watch, but Neamani, who was standing by me, half apologized for their conduct, saying they were 'tamata lialia' (fools), but that it was Vaka Viti (Fiji fashion). The rest

148

of us kept along the ridge of the hills, Tevita borrowing
my glasses every few minutes to look out for
an enemy or a good-looking taro patch. We passed
close to the site of Vatu Mali, marked now only by
the brown colour of the ground, and one tall house-
post which had escaped the flames. We reached
the river (Singatoka) at its junction with another
stream, the *Wai Tambu Thake* (Wai Tambu Thake=
Water forbidden to go higher); the river was very
low, running often in two or three channels over a
broad stony bed. The men waded across easily,
but as there was one deep pool where the rivers
met, I had a bathe in it, and then Tevita and I,
getting as much shade as we could from a clump of
rank-looking grass, sat on the burning shingle of
the river-bed whilst the men made off into the
plantations round about to collect the food. Two
of the enemy were seen on a hill over by Tatumba,
a friendly village, and we could hear the villagers
beating an alarm on their lali, so a messenger was
sent off to see what was the matter, and an answer
came back that a number of Tevoro had been annoy-
ing the village during the morning, but they had
made off on catching sight of our force. I could
not understand the messenger, and as no interpreter
was with me, I did not make out exactly what had
happened until I got back to the camp.

" The men were not long in the plantations, as
their luck was bad; there were no yams, and most
of the taro was too young for food. They roasted
a couple of bananas for my lunch, and then as soon

as all the men had come back, we followed the river down for more than a mile. Here I found the benefit of my thick boots, for the burning sand and pebbles scorched the bare feet of the natives, so that every now and then they all set off at a run to cool them in the water. We then recrossed the river and hunted through another plantation of very large extent, where the men were a little more successful. But Tevita was grumbling all the way home, for Neamani and his Taukais, with their better knowledge of the country, had managed to carry off double as much as the sotias. But he only found fault from the love of having something to grumble at, as the Nasauthoko villages have behaved wonderfully well in the matter of supplying the camp with food, and though hard up for it themselves, I have no doubt that half the taro carried off to-day will eventually find its way into camp."

Here my letter ends abruptly, for my leg became so bad that I had to be sent back to the coast on Olive's horse, the only horse in the island, for I could not put my foot to the ground. My native guard called the horse " na puaca levu " (the big pig), and would keep feeling its ribs, and asking if it was good to eat. A hurried postscript dated Nasova, 5th July, says, " My leg is quite well now, but I am awfully tired this morning as I have been up nearly all night writing and copying despatches".

So ended my connection with the little war which was most successfully carried out by the native police. What fighting there was fell to the lot of Knollys, Arthur Gordon and Dr MacGregor.

On the same date I wrote from Nasova to my sister, " The Governor came back last night, and to my surprise brought Gordon with him. The explanation was satisfactory. Gordon's men had completely smashed up the Quali Mari tribes with very small loss to themselves. They took eight hundred prisoners, including women and children, and all the ring-leaders were caught. I envy Gordon his luck, but have come in for a turn in a different way. Captain Havelock,[1] the Colonial Secretary, is leaving, and I get the appointment as Acting Colonial Secretary and Receiver-General, and become a member of the Executive and Legislative Councils. Whether I get the whole salary of £500 a year or whether Havelock draws half for the first three months, I am not sure yet. Anyhow, it is a place worth getting, and after the Chief Justice and the Officer commanding the troops I am the biggest swell in the Colony, and the whole of the administrative work is done through me. Of course I know that the appointment is not likely to be permanent, but I think I have every chance of holding it for a year, and by that time I hope to get something I should like under the High Commission.

" The Governor thanked me very heartily for the work I had already done for him, and told me that without flattery he must say that he did not know what it was to have a good Private Secretary

[1] Later Sir Arthur Havelock, Governor of Ceylon and Madras.

L

until I had come to him. I sigh when I think that I shall have to give up my scheme of six months ruralizing among the natives, but of course this is far too good a chance to let slip in favour of schemes of my own.

"This is between ourselves. It was an odd coincidence that when the Governor left for Viti Levu on his last trip, as I was not able to go with him, he took Charles Eyre, who is the son of Governor Eyre of Jamaica notoriety, to act as his Private Secretary, and his other companion was our new Chief Justice, Mr Gorrie, the Counsel for the Prosecution in Governor Eyre's trial! Could he have had two stranger companions, when he had to shoot and hang natives who had committed atrocities? He sent both his companions away on different expeditions through the country, when he saw the work that was before him, and, I think very wisely, would have no one but Arthur Gordon and the interpreter who conducted the trials present at the executions."

Just at this time we suffered a severe loss in the wreck of the *Fitzroy*, our only Government steamer and means of communication. I was alone at Nasova when the news came that she had gone ashore on a reef off the coast of Viti Levu. Luckily there was no loss of life, and most of the things on board had been saved, but I had to decide what measures should be taken, and did what proved to be right in abandoning the vessel to the underwriters, although she was only insured for £3,000 and had cost the

Colony £6,000. I managed to charter a trading
steamer to carry on the necessary communications,
until another vessel could be purchased in Australia.

From now on I was steadily at work at Nasova
until November, when I accompanied the Governor
in H.M.S. *Nymphe*, on a visit to several of the Windward Islands, and then on to the great meeting of
chiefs at Wai Kava on Vanua Levu. From a
picturesque point of view the meeting was a failure,
as the native town had no good rara (lawn). My
principal remembrance is of huge piles of mats and
masi, and innumerable pigs and turtle roasted whole.
Tui Thakau's train of masi, worn when he came
to meet the Governor, was eight yards broad and
of enormous length, seventy or more yards (it may
have been much longer), held out by his followers
behind him. After he had made a speech of welcome,
and presented some whale's teeth, the train was
dropped, and he walked away without it. Many
other chiefs went through the same ceremony according to their rank; the pile of masi left at the end
was enormous. Then a great roll of masi covered
with mats was presented. It took about a hundred
men to carry it, and the roll was twenty feet long
and three feet six high when lying on the ground.
Of course all these presents were afterwards divided
up, and given to the visitors, who had some of them
come long distances to attend the Council.

The thing that pleased me most was a canoe
race we got up : it really was a most beautiful sight.
About twenty canoes started, and the start was

perfect; their great balloon-like mat sails all went up together when the gun fired, and they got away without a single foul. The canoe I was in was the largest, and, had she been skilfully handled, should have won. But, according to Fiji fashion, the chief who had travelled in her to the meeting had, immediately on landing at Wai Kava, presented her to his host, Tui Thakau, and he had made her a present to some one else, so she had a new crew who did not know her sailing qualities. Only two or three canoes could weather the point of the reef, so the others made a dash for it through the breakers. It was such a pretty sight to see them running through. There was no real danger, as the sea was not high, and there were so many canoes about. Only one got swamped, and her crew soon baled her out and set her to rights again. My canoe got through all right without touching the coral. As usual in Fiji racing, almost all went the wrong course, but luckily the winning canoe not only went the right course, but beat the others hollow; so there was no dispute.

At the end of the year it was arranged that Lady Gordon and the children should go to New Zealand, so as to escape the hot weather in Fiji. I knew that Mr Thurston was eventually to have my place as Colonial Secretary, and it seemed to be a good time for making the change. The Governor wanted to keep me as Private Secretary, and make me Treasurer as well, so as to give me a seat on the Executive Council, but this was not likely to work

well, and as I needed a change of climate it was
finally decided that I should accompany Lady
Gordon to New Zealand, and we caught the mail
steamer at Kandavu and arrived at Auckland on
the last day of the year (1876).

CHAPTER XII

NEW ZEALAND

After settling Lady Gordon in a hotel at Auckland I went in an excursion steamer to Kawau, Sir George Grey's island home in the bay, about twenty miles north of Auckland. As it was a pouring wet day and the house and garden was overrun by trippers, I did not see the place to advantage. Sir George was very civil, and asked Lady Gordon and the children to come there as soon as possible, and extended his invitation to me ; but as the house would be very full for a time, and I wanted to see something of the country, I deferred my visit until later on, and on the 5th January, 1877, I took passage in a coasting steamer for Tauranga, about sixty miles south of Auckland. There I hired a horse and guide for a forty-two-mile ride to Ohinimotu. The first thirteen miles was through open bracken-covered land, except where the soil is so poor that even fern will not grow, and one sometimes sees a patch of tussock grass, so coarse that the horses will hardly touch it. Nothing seems to thrive on such land except the pigs, and they manage to grow fat on fern roots. A few English weeds such as dock and dandelion one sees sometimes by the roadside. Then we rode for eighteen miles through the most beautiful forest I have ever seen outside the tropics. The trees were very large, and usually had small leaves; and the undergrowth, which is almost impenetrable, was for the most part made up of large-leaved plants and creepers and parasites innumerable. Tree ferns of course, abound. After getting through the forest, we could see the lake country spread out before us, undulating and fern-covered, with hardly any forest and not very attractive-looking, and here and there one could see steam rising from the hot springs. A few hours' ride brought us to Ohinimotu, where I put up at a small inn, and at once walked off to the edge of the lake, only a few yards distant, and had a swim in the warm water, which effectually took off the stiffness from my long ride.

After bathing, my guide and I strolled round the native village, which is situated on a point running out into the lake (Roto Rua). There is only one really good house (houses are called "Whares" here), used as a sort of Council Hall and general loafing place. It is semi-European on the outside, but the porch and interior are covered with grotesque carving. The village did not look as habitable as an ordinary Fijian village. Maoris in all states of dress and undress were loafing about in dirty European clothes; a large blanket seems to be the most fashionable costume, since it is easy to get rid of when one wants to squat in a hot spring or take a swim in the lake. We were hailed by three Maori damsels who had a large basket of wild cherries, and wished us to come and share them. My guide speaks Maori like a native, so our conversation got on splendidly. They were fairly good-looking girls, but horribly dressed, and their hair would have been improved by a little brushing. Two of them were tatooed on the under-lip and chin, the only part of the face that is decorated in the women. Their complexions were about the same as the Tongans', but they show more red colour through the skin, which is a great improvement. The men are often tattooed all over the face—not a bit like Tongan or Fijian tattooing, but great deep-cut blue lines and curves, the patterns very graceful, whatever the general result may be.

In the evening I went for another bathe. That seemed to be the fashionable bathing time, as a whole circle of men were sitting up to their chins in the hot water, smoking and chatting away quite happily, and some of the women were swimming about. And one damsel with a short black pipe in her mouth swam up to me to say, " Kua Koe " (How are you ?) and have a look at the Pakeha (white man). Bathing dresses are not in fashion after tea.

It is beyond description delicious rolling about in the warm mud; it is softer than down, and not a bit sticky or unpleasant, unless by chance you put your foot where a hot spring is oozing up, and that does make one swear. One can drive one's arm right down through the mud as far as it will go, and on drawing it out, not one atom of mud adheres to it.

About an hour of it was enough for me, but the natives seemed inclined to make a night of it, and on a moonlight night, with a little less wind blowing, I think I should have been much inclined to do the same. As it was, the wind was so cold that, as soon as I was out of the water, I ran off to my bed. By moving a little distance from the shore, one can get water of any temperature one likes, as the hot springs are near the margin of the lake. I was told that formerly there was a geyser of great power in the middle of the little bay in which I had been bathing, but that it had ceased to act for some years.

The next morning my guide returned with the horses to Tauranga, and I engaged fresh horses and a Maori, Tautere by name, to take me to Rotomahana. Tautere turned out to be an extremely good fellow, and we got on capitally. The following two days I spent on the borders of the two lakes, Roto Rua and Roto Iti, sleeping at a little native village named Tahake. The country was not very interesting, much the same as I had already passed through. At Tahake there is a very fine large whare, covered with carvings beautifully executed, but horribly indecent. Tautere said the natives were " very mean Maoris". There was some difficulty in getting into this big house, as it was apparently unoccupied, and the old gentleman who had charge of the key was away, and had, as we were told, probably planted the key somewhere before starting. On the fence surrounding the house were the remains of part of a famous Maori war canoe, of which the side pieces were of great length and elaborately carved. From what was left of it, I should think that it must have been cut out of two huge trees pieced together in the middle, and would have held about 250 men. Tautere told me that a man to whom he acted as guide had offered £100 apiece for the side pieces, but the Maoris would not part with them. I did not think it was much good looking for the key, and began to try to get into the house through the single window. However, the whole village turned out on the hunt, and in about half an hour after searching all round the house, the key was found hidden away under an old bit of matting.

We took our saddles into the house and were just beginning to think about supper, and Tautere had pulled a packet of tea out of his pocket, when another Maori rushed at him and cried, " Taboo ", and then the mystery of the deserted appearance of the house was explained. A Chief of high rank had died, and his body was lying there to " dry ", previous to the bones being scraped and hidden away. As the house was full of rubbish and odds and ends of clothing, boxes, etc., I had not noticed a large box covered with black cloth, in which the chief was " drying ". Now any food taken into a house where a dead body is lying is tabooed for ever, so I had all the tea to myself, as even my much Europeanized guide refused to touch it that night, although he did drink a little, freely diluted with milk, the next morning. Luckily for Tautere the rest of the food had been left outside the house, so when some potatoes had been cooked (potatoes seem to be the principal food of the Maoris) we had our supper on the grass. The natives then asked me where I would like to sleep, and offered no objection to my sleeping in the big whare, and further mentioned that I could have it to myself, as no one else would dare to sleep there, and that the body was not " high ", and it seemed to me preferable to the dirty crowded huts of the villagers. After supper some of the people came into the whare to have a smoke, and we had a long talk. They were delighted to examine my knife and a few other things I had with me, and brought some of their baskets and carved work for me to look at in return. Altogether we had a very pleasant evening, and then they went off to their own huts to sleep.

I found I was not to be quite alone, as an old lady was left to watch the corpse. This watching is supposed to be a mark of great affection for the deceased chief, and usually falls to the lot of one of his near kindred, and the watcher becomes very much taboo indeed, and is not even allowed to feed herself ; everything has to be put into her mouth by attendants, and this goes on for months and months, until the body is quite dry, and the bones ready for scraping. It is very seldom, I was told, that the body is kept in a large whare, usually a small house is built on purpose to hold it.

There was a large wooden bedstead in the house covered with a mat, on which I slept, and slept very soundly after my long ride, although I was dimly conscious of many fleas, and in the morning I found that I was bitten all over. Tautere told me it was lucky I had slept in the whare, for the hut to which he went was so full of fleas that he could get no sleep at all. After a bathe in the lake and a good breakfast of crayfish and potatoes and tabooed tea, we rode back to Ohinimotu, passing some curious hot springs and a small lake on the way, and a picturesque lake among the hills called Roto Kawau.

The next morning we started for Roto Mahana. About ten miles' ride through fern country brought us to Wairoa, a village with a small inn kept by an Englishman called Brown, evidently a gentleman.[1] I had a long chat with him, and he told me that since his arrival in New Zealand he had tried his hand at everything, and a week before had turned publican. I must say he seemed very happy over it. We had to leave our horses here and cross the end of the Roto Terawera in a canoe. The natives, who were a most disreputable-looking lot, were fighting among themselves about the privilege of taking travellers to see Roto Mahana and the Terraces. The crew engaged by Tautere were not allowed to take us, and at one time it seemed as if their squabbling would end in our not being able to go at all. However, at last, with Brown's help a crew was engaged consisting of one hunchback, two old women and a boy, and we scrambled down the steep hill to

---

[1] I was told that afterwards he distinguished himself as a soldier in South Africa, and was known as " Maori Brown ".

the lake at dawn, and got away before anyone else was about.

Terawera is the prettiest lake I have yet seen, with well-wooded banks and steep cliffs; as the name implies, it is always rather warm.

All the land here, as indeed nearly all the land we passed through, since leaving Tauranga, is the property of the Maoris, and the few inns and stables are built on patches leased by them to Europeans. The terraces of Roto Mahana are claimed by each of two sections of a tribe; and that is the origin of the present squabble. Government has over and over again tried to buy land from them, but the natives will not sell, and are contented with fleecing the unfortunate tourists who come to see the Terraces.

The canoe we went in was, like all Maori canoes, merely a large dug-out of great length. My crew were not very active, and our progress after the first spurt was slow, and Tautere did most of the work. As we passed a small bare rock at the end of a point of land, each native threw on it a sprig of fern to appease the spirit of the lake. We stopped about an hour under a woody bank, while the crew hunted for wild honey, and at last brought back a large tin billy full of it, and as much more in the comb as they could carry. This did not improve our pace, as they were continually stopping to feast on it.

About two o'clock we reached the end of the lake, and left our canoe in a creek near some native huts. There were several hot springs round the

edge of this part of the lake, and in a basin formed
by one of them, close to the side of a hut, a poor boy
was lying. He had been suffering from some disease
of the hip-joint, and found sitting in the hot water
eased his pain. When his friends moved him out
he had fainted, so they put him back again, until
at last he had got to live in the water, and when
I saw him (with the exception of a few minutes
about once a fortnight, when they moved him to
clear out the pool) he had been living in the water
continuously for eleven months. He was a nice-
looking boy, but dreadfully thin, and I do not think
he would survive the treatment much longer. A roof
of reeds had been built over him, and supports
placed under him, so that he could lie comfortably,
and keep his head out of water.

It is quite possible to go by canoe from Terawera
to Roto Mahana ; but as it was the breeding season
of the ducks the Maoris allowed no canoes to be taken
to the lake, so we had to walk a few miles overland, crossing one small river on the way where
we stopped to bathe, the water being as usual tepid.
Then we climbed a hill and came in sight of the
White Terrace. We slept that night in a little shack
just big enough for us all to crawl into. I rolled
myself in a blanket in the corner, but finding it
very hot, managed to turn over, when a little jet
of steam came up where I had been lying. Any
book you have read about New Zealand will have
had a description of the Terraces, so I will not weary
you with another. They originated, I should think,
as geysers spouting from the side of the hill, about

two hundred yards from the lake. The water is of a milky-blue colour, and on evaporation leaves a thickish deposit of silica in some combination or other, not so hard but much whiter than that of the Icelandic Geysers.

The pool at the top, which I take to be the original geyser, is about one hundred and fifty feet across, intensely blue and always boiling. One takes a header into the lowest pool near the lake, swims across, climbs up the first parapet, dives into the next pool, and goes on up, each pool getting hotter and hotter, until near the top one can go no further without being boiled, and one slides and swims down through pool after pool until one reaches the lake again. We spent the day swimming about the pools, and then went to see the Red Terraces on the other side of the lake, which are not quite so large as the White Terraces. The colour comes from some deposit in the silica, but the effect is just as though a huge fire, blazing on the other side of the lake, were throwing a red reflection on the terraces.[1]

On my return from Rotomahana I went to stay at Kawau with Sir George Grey. I hardly knew the Gordon children again, they were so much improved by the few weeks' change of climate. Kawau is a delightful place, an island of about six thousand acres, naturally very picturesque ; and Sir George has improved it much by judicious clearing and by planting English trees, which thrive most wonderfully,

[1] Both Terraces were a few years later destroyed by a volcanic eruption, but I have been told that they are again forming.

and grow twice as fast as they do at home ; round the house he has collections of trees and shrubs from all parts of the world. The island is full of game, wild cattle, kangaroo, wallaby, deer, pheasants, peafowl, quail, duck and pigeons, all except the latter introduced. The deer-stalking is first-rate, but the kangaroo and wallaby are so confiding that they almost come to look down the muzzle of my gun, and I can't shoot them ! I left my rifle in Fiji, and one I have borrowed is almost useless, so I do most of my hunting with a field-glass, watching the animals come out of the woods to feed, but my long walks have put me in splendid condition. Numbers of tree-wallaby from New Guinea live in the bush quite close to the house ; they are such pretty little fellows.

Sir George Grey is in bad health, but he is capital company, and knows everybody worth knowing, political, social, literary or scientific. He has a capital library, and in the house there are (mixed, I must own, with a good deal of rubbish) valuable curiosities and works of art from all parts of the world. There is capital sea fishing in the bay, and the beach just in front of the house is covered with oysters, and we got very clever at opening them by a blow on the hinge with a stone, and feasting at our pleasure.

The children were delighted to see me again, but I noticed that Sir George, who liked attention from the children, distinctly resented it if they came to play with me when he was present. It was so marked and curious an attitude that I called Lady Gordon's attention to it, who said she had already noticed it, and we agreed that I had better not notice the children when he was present. It was such a trifling matter, but I feel sure it was typical of the failing which blemished an otherwise great career. He was evidently cursed by a jealous temperament, and this overshadowed his brilliant abilities, and marked the quarrels and controversies with generals, chief-justices and others who served with him. Although he posed as a democrat, he was an autocart by nature, and could stand no opposition or rivalry. He had governed Western Australia, New Zealand twice, and South Africa twice, and while I was staying with him, we heard the news of Sir Theophilus Shepstone's annexation of the Transvaal; and he got me to take down the volumes of his old South African Despatches, and read them to him. Certainly, he was the most attractive and interesting man I have ever met.

CHAPTER XIII

THE KING COUNTRY

There was at this time still a part of the North Island known as the King Country, where the Maoris kept their independence under King Tawihau, and where the Queen's writ did not run, and where no Europeans were allowed except a few malefactors who had escaped and crawled over the border. As I was anxious to go and see the Maoris in their own country, Sir George, who was always on the best of terms with the Maoris, gave me letters to the King, and some of the principal Chiefs, and by keeping my intentions quite dark and making no fuss about it I hoped to get smuggled over the border unmolested. When I got near the border-line at Alexandra, I put myself in the hands of Mr Duffas, a storekeeper to whom I had a letter; he seemed a nice fellow and ready to help me. He took me off at once to Major Te Whero, the head friendly chief in Government employment, to whom also I had a letter.

Te Whero set to work directly, and sent messengers across the border to announce my arrival. Te Whero paid me a visit the next morning, and confidently told Mr Duffas that he had been thinking over my

arrival all night, and had come to the conclusion
that as we had settled our native disturbances so
quickly in Fiji, he felt sure that the Queen had
sent me to the Maoris to find out why it was that
the same settlement could not be come to in New
Zealand, and that he had written to the King's
Chief Minister to tell him so! This was a great
blow, but Mr Duffas told me that they were sure
to suspect that there was something up, and it
was as well they should think that as anything
else. I was, however, most anxious that they should
not think I had come for any political purpose, as
it might lead to trouble.

The following morning a half-caste named Turner
made his appearance, who was to act as my guide
and interpreter. He brought a very good hack of
Te Whero's for me to ride, and we set off immediately
for Te Kopua, where Manuwheri, one of the chiefs
to whom I had brought letters, and Tawihau's chief
adviser, was staying. A mile's ride brought us to
the boundary line, and it was a further seven miles
to Te Kopua. The country was partly under cultivation, wheat and potatoes being the chief crops, and
here and there one saw small wooden houses belong-
ing to half-castes.

We had to swim our horses across the river, while
the natives ferried us across in a canoe. Te Kopua
I found to consist of a few wretched shanties, in
one of which I found the chief Manuwheri. He
was an old man with a much tattooed face, and was
lying on his mat wrapped up in a blanket of many

colours. He turned out of his hut to shake hands
with me, and told me I was welcome. Then I held
a regular levée, all the people crowding into the
hut to shake hands with me, and sitting huddled up
anyhow, without paying the slightest attention or
respect to Manuwheri, who was hustled up into a
corner and seemed quite content with the arrangement. (I should like to see a Fijian Chief treated
like that, one would have heard some remarks about
the mothers and fathers of the intruders, neither
complimentary nor true.) The first remark made
to me was that I was too young to come to see them,
which made me think I was looked upon as a sort
of ambassador. After that we had a long talk about
Fiji, the little war, the people, etc., in which they
seemed to take the greatest interest ; and they were
delighted with a number of photographs of Fijians
and Tongans which I happened to have with me
(I had shewn these photographs the night before
to Major Te Whero, and the only remark he made
was when looking at some of the rather scantily-
clothed women, " Ah ! Very much like the ladies
at the Government House balls ". The Maori women
are very careful to cover their breasts.) It seemed
as though they would never end asking me questions
about Fiji and the other islands of the Pacific, wanting
to know the distance of one group from the other,
and then they told me about their own migration
from Hawaii.

At last the visitors moved off, and I was not sorry
for it, as the house could not have measured more

than fifteen feet by eight, and we were very close packed inside, and there was a crowd round the door. Manuwheri's daughter, who must have been a very handsome woman when younger, then brought the dinner, consisting of boiled pork and potatoes, served up in two flax baskets, no plates, knives or forks, every one eating with his fingers, one pocket-knife being used to cut up the meat. Then, hearing a great din from the hammering of iron bars on kerosene tins, I asked what it meant, and was told it was Sunday, and those were the bells for church! I made it Thursday, but the Maoris had started a new religion, and I was told that the King had decided that four Sundays in the month was too many, so they had a Sunday every ten days.

After further conversation and a smoke, one of the chiefs asked me to come to church, as the evening service was about to begin, and of course I said yes. The church was merely another shanty of the same appearance as Manuwheri's house, but rather larger. A small piece of matting had been spread for me to sit upon, and the rest of the congregation, not more than twenty in all, sat round on the earthen floor with their backs against the walls of the house. The service was not very elaborate, and there appeared to be no priest. One man stood up and muttered what I supposed was a prayer, and then broke into a dismal chant in which all joined; then the man sat down, and another went through the same performance, women as well as men taking their turn. The whole service did not take more than

a quarter of an hour. One of the men turned round
to me and said, " Those are the songs our forefathers
sang, when they came from Hawaii ". As soon as
the service was over, some one produced a dirty
pack of cards, and all set to work to play Loo, the
stake one lucifer match each. Now it happened
that I had played a good deal at Loo, and after a
few rounds I noticed that the chief sitting next to
me held a good hand, and was about to lead the
wrong card, so I took his hand from him and played
the cards for him, and won two tricks, which he
would have lost, had he played as he intended. He
was perfectly delighted at winning, and stood my
friend all through the bad half-hour that followed,
for soon afterwards they sent all the women out of
the house, and two or three of the chiefs subjected
me to a long and not too pleasant cross-examination.
They would not believe I had not come on some
special mission, and were most anxious to know
what Sir George had sent me to say to them. At
last I think I convinced them that I had not come on
political business. They seemed rather disappointed,
telling me that Sir George should have known better
than to have sent me, if he had nothing to say to
them, that had I been a creeping thing come among
them they would have taken no notice of me, and
I could have gone where I liked, for they could not
take the trouble to look after loafers ; but that a
gentleman should come to see them, with no particular
object in view, they could not understand. As I
had come so far they would make me welcome, but

that I was to tell Sir George not to send anyone to them except on business ; and that, thinking I had come on business, they had sat up the whole of the previous night holding a meeting to arrange what to say to me.

I went off to sleep at the house of a half-caste, which they said I would find a great deal more comfortable than their whares.

The next morning I went round to several places where the Maoris were at work reaping wheat, and went through much hand-shaking and conversation ; one old lady insisted on going through the native salutation of rubbing noses with me. Luckily my native companions took a good deal of the trouble of talking to newcomers on themselves, for they were most energetic in retailing all the stories I had told them the day before about Fiji.

In the afternoon I paid another visit to Manu-wheri, whom I found alone, and asked him about visiting the King, but he strongly objected to my going on any further, answering all my suggestions with " I advise you to go back ". The King, he said, had told him to take no notice of caterpillars; but I came in holding my head up. I told him that, as I had no political mission, and had paid them a visit merely with a desire to see something of their country and mode of life, I should not attempt to go further ; but at the same time I felt greatly disappointed at not having seen the King, and lived for a few weeks among them. However, the old man would not hear of my going any further, and told me I had already ridden through much of his country on my way there, country which had been taken by the white men, and he went off into a long story about the power and position of the Maoris in the old days. So after about an hour's talk with him I saddled my horse and rode back to Alexandra.

When I got back to Auckland I met a friend at the Club, who said, " I know where you have been. There was a good deal of excitement among the settlers near the border, when they heard that some-one had ridden over into the King Country, and one of them bribed the maid-servant at Alexandra to search some things you had left behind there, and she found out your name ".

After another visit to Sir George at the Kawau, I went down to the South Island and stayed with George Reeves, an old Cambridge friend, near Nelson, and rode over the Mokotap Pass to Havelock and Picton. At a very lonely spot in the narrowest part of the track I saw the skulls and bones of the horses shot by some bushrangers who, after shooting their horses, had robbed the riders and held them prisoners until they had collected enough loot, and then got clean away.

Nelson I found a most attractive little town, with a good climate and pleasant surroundings. From Nelson I went by sea through the French Pass to Wellington, and cannot say that I was at all impressed by the magnificence of what they call the Empire City. Brick and stone buildings will not stand the earth-quakes, and I was in the hope that a city avowedly

built of wood might be quaint and picturesque.
But alas! the buildings are usually run up on
a wooden framework and then covered with corrugated iron; then a front made to look as much like
stone as possible is added, all sham and pretence.
My name had been put down for the Club, but Lord
Normanby asked me to stay with him at Government
House, where I spent a very pleasant week, and
then they very kindly gave me a passage back to
Auckland in the Government steamer *Hinemoa,*
which I had to myself, arriving in Auckland just in
time to meet Lady Gordon and sail in the mail
steamer for Kandavu.

As the *Fitzroy* had been wrecked, and there was
no other steamer available, the Governor had sent
a forty-ton ketch *The Barb* to Kandavu to meet
us as the only means of transport. And in this
our party, consisting of Lady Gordon, two children,
Miss Gordon Cumming, two nurses, Colonel Pratt
and myself, had to travel the hundred miles to Suva,
and arrived there on 17th April. Luckily the weather
was fine, and there was a good breeze, so we did
the journey in twenty-four hours. Lady Gordon
called it twenty-four hours of misery.

While we were in New Zealand there was another
loss to our Fiji party, in the death of Mrs McGregor,
the wife of our Chief Medical Officer.

Two days after our arrival in Suva letters came
to say that a deputation of chiefs was on its way
from Samoa to petition the Governor for British
protection; and the Governor and I immediately

175

returned to Levuka. The chiefs arrived on the 21st April; a house was prepared for them at Draimba, and on the 23rd we had an official reception at Nasova. The chiefs did not appear to know what they wanted; and since the Commissions as High Commissioner and Consul-General had not reached the Governor, he had no power to act, and could do no more than say that the petition would be forwarded to the Queen.

Then the chiefs were sent off to Bau to be entertained by Thakombau, so that they might find out for themselves how much truth there was in the stories that had been circulated in Samoa about the "slavery and ill-treatment of the Fijian chiefs".

The failure to issue the Commissions had all along caused great inconvenience. It had been a promise to the Governor, when he accepted the Government of Fiji, that he should also be High Commissioner under the Order in Council for the Western Pacific, and Consul-General, and that there should be no Consuls within his jurisdiction except those appointed by himself. Yet the F.O. had appointed Mr Liardet Consul in Samoa, and that gentleman had not even sent home his despatches under flying seal to Sir Arthur, as he had been instructed by the F. O. to do, but had taken an independent line of his own and made a sad mess of it. So the Governor thought it advisable that I should go to England to endeavour to hurry up the Commissions, to explain the financial position of the Colony and see to many other matters which needed attention. My instructions were very short, very liberal, and practically placed the Governor's resignation in my hands, if I found his wishes were not acceded to.

CHAPTER XIV

TO ENGLAND AND FIJI AGAIN

I sailed for home on the 11th May, 1877, by way of Hawaii, San Francisco and New York, and reached England on the 22nd July.

It was an unfortunate time to arrive, as the Transvaal had just been annexed, and Parliament was busy over the South African Bill. Members were anxious to get away for their holidays; Government Offices were very busy, and the Russo-Turkish War was occupying everyone's attention. However, I had a very interesting time, met many distinguished people, and among other engagements had breakfast alone with Mr Gladstone; but I got most assistance from Lord Selbourne. No doubt I worried both the Colonial and Foreign Offices a good deal, but at last I was successful in getting both Commissions sent to Sir Arthur. At the very last there was a hitch over the Great Seal. Mr Herbert tried to persuade me to start for Fiji, saying that the seal would be sent after me, but I refused to budge. "The Seal will be a very heavy package for you to carry across Europe," said Mr Herbert. But I would not let that alter my determination. It was a heavy metal stamping seal, and when finally it was ready I asked that it might be packed in an official mail bag, and freely sealed with Colonial Office and Foreign Office Seals, so that it might avoid examination at Custom Houses. I stayed one night in Paris, I think, to go to the theatre to see Croisette in the "Sphinx". When I arrived at the station the next night I found the train crowded, but I made play with my mail-bag and its seals, and interviewed the station master, regretting my inability to speak his language, but managing to impress on him that I was carrying despatches. Then every one was hat in hand, and I was given a coupé to myself. Just as the train was starting, the door was opened and the station master appeared with some other excited officials, and asked, " Would Monsieur be so good as to allow a lady to have a seat in his carriage, as there was not another seat vacant in the train ? " Who the lady was I never knew, but evidently someone of importance by the fuss they made about her. As soon as we started she began to talk to me, and I expressed my regret that I did not speak French. But she said, " I see you are reading a French newspaper ! And if you can read a French paper, you know enough to talk to me ". And she insisted on keeping up a conversation, or rather a monologue, until she left the train about midnight, and I got some sleep.

I travelled by way of Brindisi, Suez and Galle to Melbourne, where I heard that it would be some days before the steamer left Sydney for Fiji. So

I left the steamer at Melbourne with the intention of going overland to Sydney.

Extracts from letter to my sister—

"My name had been put down for the Melbourne Club by wire from Adelaide. I left a card next day at Government House, and received a letter from Sir George Bowen, regretting my short stay, and asking me to dinner that night and the next. I had heard so much about Sir George in Queensland and elsewhere that I was curious to meet him. Lady Bowen and the children were at some watering-place, so we had plenty of chance for a good talk, and he unburdened himself to me on many topics, including the present political crisis in Victoria (which is very serious, and Sir George has, I think, put his foot in it badly), his disagreement with Sir Hercules Robinson, and many other subjects on which he ought never to have spoken to a stranger. I met several friends at the Club, but could not accept their invitations, as I was bound to Sir George. He had asked me to stay at Government House, but this I was able to get out of. On Sunday I went for a walk with him in the Botanical Gardens. They are really very pretty indeed and very extensive.

"The new Government House is a huge place : ball-room to hold between two and three thousand persons, reception rooms in proportion ; a beautiful site, but the house externally hideous. The interior needs much furnishing and humanizing, but an awful lot of money has been spent on it already.

"On Monday morning I started for Albury, about eight hours by rail, rested there until midnight, then left in the coach to meet the New South Wales Railroad. My fellow-travellers were not over pleasant: squabbled all night long about the box-seat, one man wanting to fight the driver. Very dreary country, bush road, and awfully hot and dusty when the sun rose. Coached all day, and arrived that evening at that celebrated spot Wagga Wagga. I can now quite understand the claimant's reason for making up the Tichborne story. Anything would be preferable to spending a summer in that rising township, except Milbank. Slept at Wagga and coached the next day to Cootamundra. Country a little better, but dreadfully dried up every-where. One of the passengers was so drunk that, after being annoyed with him for two stages, we conspired with the driver and left him behind at one of the wayside publics, fast asleep on the flat of his back, to be picked up when sober. Arrived at Cootamundra about six o'clock, half an hour to feed, and then all night in a crowded train to Sydney.

"I stayed at the Australian Club for two days, dined at Government House, and heard all the news from Lady Bob, then sailed in the *Wentworth*, a a small, slow steamer, for Fiji. Think of the liberality of the Steamship Company! They have given me a free passage to Fiji, and a free pass on their steamers for a year. I never knew what my perquisites were before! We arrived in Port at Levuka on 21st January, and I was very well received. I am better satisfied with the result of my trip home, now that I have returned, than I was when leaving England. The Colonial Office people have written very civil things about me, and the Governor seems pleased with what I have done."

A week after my return I was appointed a Lands Commissioner, and went off to the mouth of the Navua river, on the south coast of Viti Levu, to try land claims. Never have I had such a baking as on that journey. I suppose I was soft after my trip home. The place appointed for the court was at a village at the mouth of the river, where the claimants and their witnesses had assembled, but when I tried to hold a court the next day the mosquitoes were in such swarms that, by general consent, we moved some miles up the river to Wai Wanga, the village of one Harry Danford, better known as " Harry the Jew ". He gained this name from some yarn about selling a watch, and not on account of his birth, although his mother was an Italian Jewess—at least, he tells me that he thinks she was, but I don't think he was quite clear about it. He was not quite certain about his Christian name, when I came to swear him as a witness, and I had to write it down; but he had been in Fiji over fifty years, and had never been known as anything but " Harry ". He ran away from a whaler at Tonga, and came in a canoe to Fiji. Not so much was thought of a voyage of two or three hundred miles out to sea in a native canoe in those days. Harry's house is in a charming situation on the river-bank, and is fairly comfortable (barring mosquitoes). It consists of one big room, forty feet by twenty, and this serves as bedroom and living-room for us all and for my court-room as well in the daytime. In the evenings I heard all sorts of stories of the old days in the mountains, where Harry was as long as six years without seeing a white face, and was living on the best of terms with the most ferocious cannibals. Harry, being a sailor and a handy man, was invaluable to a tribe always at war, as he understood the mystery of the locks of guns ; and when the white men at last began to penetrate into the country he knew how to talk to them, and to get powder and lead in exchange for tracts of land, and he could tell what the papers meant to which the chiefs were asked to put their mark. That he behaved fairly and honestly to his native friends I fully believe, and his old age, as chief of a native village, with a good bit of land of his own, a native wife and family, and plenty of natives to look after him and make him comfortable, is, I should think, much to be preferred to a " Sailors' Infirmary ", which would most likely have been his fate had he stuck to his profession.

I found Harry to be an interesting and pleasant old fellow, and when I left he made me a present of one of his half-caste sons, aged about sixteen, who stayed with me until I left the Pacific, when I returned him to his father. The mosquitoes were still bad, but nothing like they were at the mouth of the river. I stayed at Wai Wanga about a fortnight, holding courts every day, and heard most of the land-claims in the district. It was interesting work, although I was a good deal worried by claimants who thought they knew something about law ; the real lawyers were much more moderate and sensible. My advice to people buying land from natives in an unsettled country would be always to buy by natural land-marks, and, unless they are trained surveyors, never to use a compass. Much of the trouble in Fiji came from deeds where compass bearings were wrongly stated. One man bought land running a mile inland from the coast in a north-westerly direction, omitted the side bearings of the plot, and came down to the coast in a south-easterly direction, so he had apparently bought a straight line—length without breadth ! Of course there were many interesting cases of tribal rights, and the rights of vendors to sell land, and some questions about the names of natural land-marks. In one case I had to deal with there was a written deed in which one boundary was stated to be the Waini Buney Swankey, and no native could identify it. The claim as advanced was a large one. Now it happened that I always went out at daybreak and fished the river running in front of the house, or wandered through the bush for an hour or so en-deavouring to learn the lie of the land, and one morning as I was returning I had to jump a small stream with muddy banks, and asked a native who was with me what it was called, and he replied,

" Na wai ni Vu ni Sawanga ", that is, " the stream of the root of the wild banana plant ". There was no doubt that this was the missing boundary, and it cut down the claim very considerably. I had an excellent interpreter in Mr Hefferman, but I found it was a great advantage knowing enough of the language to understand what a witness was saying, and being free to watch his demeanour.

The Navua river is full of fish, which rise well to a fly, and, although I could not spare more than an hour in the early morning or evening for fishing, we always had as much fish as we wanted to eat. Wild ducks too were plentiful.

When my work was over I went for a trip up the Navua river, canoeing most of the way, and had some good fly-fishing ; then a day's walk through a splendid mountain gorge took me to Namosi, one of the old mountain towns, and a most charmingly picturesque place, amid the grandest scenery I had as yet met with in Fiji.

There was a good grove of orange trees along the bank of the stream running through the village, and the forks of the branches were full of human bones—the remains of cannibal feasts ; on the village green there were two stones in the ground nine feet apart, marking the size of the body of a giant who had been eaten. I don't suppose the measurement had been very accurately taken, and I expect they stretched him a bit, but he must have been an unusually tall man for the natives to have thought it worth while to record his height. The Bure ni

Sa, or man's house, was surrounded by stones piled up against the foundation-mound, and each stone recorded the body of an enemy who had been brought into the village and eaten, when it was a privilege of the slayer to add a stone to the heap. I found Tui Namosi, the head of the district, an excellent host, and his people had been peaceful and Christian for some few years. A fork of one of the orange trees with the bones in it is now in the British Museum. I climbed up on Voma, the mountain which overhangs the town, a rough scramble for three thousand feet.

From Namosi I followed the banks of the Wai-ni-ndina to its junction with the Wai-ni-Mala, where I spent a night with Mr Carew, the Commissioner for the mountain districts. As I was strolling down to a pool in the river to bathe the next morning, I heard shouts from Carew, who sent to tell me on no account to bathe there, for a woman had been seized by a shark when wading across the end of the pool only a few days before. One did not expect to find sharks so many miles up a fresh-water river, and I have always thought they must have been tempted up in old days by the remains of cannibal feasts, for these always took place near streams.

Two days' pleasant canoeing took me down the river to Rewa Town, where I took boat and returned to Nasova. The Governor met me as I landed on the pier with the startling news that H.M.S. *Sapphire* was in harbour, and that I was to leave in her at once for Samoa! I had to beg for two days' respite to write up my land reports, hear all the Samoan news and get my instructions. It seems that while I was at Navua the Governor, having at last received his Commission as High Commissioner, had been to Samoa in H.M.S. *Sapphire*. It would take too long to go into all the complicated storm in a tea-cup that was raging in Samoa. It will be enough to say that there had been a civil war, and many of the defeated chieftains had taken refuge within the fence that surrounded the British Consulate, and their enemies threatened to cut their heads off if they put them outside; the Taimua and Faipule had possession of Mulinuú, the so-called "seat of Government", the village on the point just beyond the town of Apia, and had to be considered the " de facto " Government, although they proved themselves absolutely incapable of governing. There were a small number of disreputable white men dabbling in native politics, in hope of some profit for themselves. And there was a German Consul, Mr Weber, who was head of a branch of the great trading house of Godefroy of Hamburg, which held large plantations in Samoa, and a hopelessly incapable United States Vice-Consul, Mr Griffin. As the *Sapphire* steamed into Apia it was noticed that all flags were half mast high, for the British Consul, Mr Liardet, had died that morning. It was learnt that he had been suffering from mental disease for some time, which no doubt accounted for his extraordinary behaviour. His young wife and baby and his mother-in-law were left practically destitute in the Consulate.

There had been an incident in the previous autumn which, although altogether illegal, had a good effect. A drunken American sailor named Cochrane murdered another American named Fox. The American Consul sent Cochrane in custody on board an American vessel, the *Ada May*, for trial in the United States, but the same evening a meeting of white men presided over by an Englishman was held in Apia, and on a resolution being passed thirty men boarded the *Ada May*, seized Cochrane and hanged him to a coconut tree near the British Consulate.

Sir Arthur Gordon got on very well with Weber, who was by far the most important person in Samoa, but his attempts to come to terms with the native Government were hopeless failures. At their first meetings the deputation from the Taimua and Faipule appeared to be conciliatory and ready to accept the measures Sir Arthur proposed, but as negotiation went on they frequently changed the members of the deputation, and the work had to be done over again ; and each new member became more obstructive, until at last they announced that they would make no agreement and sign nothing. The reason given was that they had promised not to sign anything, although it was never stated to whom the promise was made. However, there was no doubt whatever that it was Griffin, the American Vice-Consul, who was directing their policy ; he refused to act in concert with Sir Arthur and Weber, and told Sir Arthur that his instructions were not to

have anything to do with native politics, but at
this very time he was living at Mulinuú in the shanty
which did service as the office of the native Government, which he said was necessary as a protection
against the British " Roughs ". Sir Arthur professed
to believe that he was instructed not to interfere
in native matters, would not discuss them with
him, and when they met they discussed English
Literature, of which Mr Griffin claimed to be a
great admirer, especially of Bulwer and his famous
play of *Childe Harold !* Weber said that he thought
Griffin was really out of his mind, but there was
some method in his madness, for he was waiting for
the return of Mamea, a Samoan who had been sent
as an envoy to Washington with a request from the
Taimua and Faipule for protection by the United
States, and this was done after they had already
asked for protection from Great Britain, and had
not yet received an answer to that petition. It was
evident that the Taimua and Faipule were merely
attempting to play off one Government against
another. Griffin then wrote to Sir Arthur, warning
him against any negotiation with Samoa, as it was
under the protection of the United States, to the
Government of which any wishes of Great Britain
should be addressed ! And he ran up the stars and
stripes above the Samoan flag at Mulinuú. Sir
Arthur's wish was to make a treaty of friendship
with Samoa, and to establish a joint municipality in
Apia, in which Weber was in agreement with him ;
but when all efforts failed, there still remained the

matter of the removal of the defeated chieftains from the yard of the Consulate, and the payment of the fine imposed for the deaths of the British Bluejackets. Sir Arthur asked for a guarantee that the lives of the chiefs should be spared, and offered easy terms of payment for the fine; but the Taimua and Faipule were obdurate, although at the last meeting Sir Arthur and Weber spent five hours in their endeavour to persuade them to come to terms. When it was certain that nothing would come from further negotiation, armed boats from the *Sapphire* took possession of the schooner *Elizabeth*, which was the property of the Samoan Government, as part payment of the fine. Then Sir Arthur re-embarked in the *Sapphire* and returned to Fiji with the *Elizabeth* in tow.

While Sir Arthur was in Samoa, Judge Gorrie, the chief justice of Fiji, held courts in Apia as Judicial Commissioner under the " Order in Council ", and sent a man named Hunt to imprisonment in Fiji for his share in the lynching of Cochrane.

It was into this turmoil, with no previous knowledge of a Consul's duties, and with my instructions dotted down on a half-sheet of notepaper, that I was suddenly launched.

CHAPTER XV

TO SAMOA AS CONSUL

I arrived at Apia, Samoa, on the 12th March, 1878. As soon as the *Sapphire* came to anchor I sent to ask the native Government to meet me.

Extract from letter to Sir Arthur Gordon—

" In compliance with my request the Taimua and Faipule appointed three o'clock on Wednesday afternoon for a meeting. Captain Murray was present at the meeting, which took place at Mulinuú point. On the flagstaff close to the house where we met, the American flag was flying over the Samoan flag, but bearing in mind your correspondence with Mr Griffin, which you showed me at Nasova, I did not think the matter worthy of any further notice.

" I delivered to the Taimua your Excellency's letter, and the letter from Lord Derby ; then after the usual civilities had passed, I read a paragraph from your last letter to them, and explained that if the terms you had offered them were accepted, the schooner *Elizabeth* would be returned to them, and I asked if they were prepared to sign the agreement. I received in reply nothing but long speeches full of excuses. I therefore requested them to reconsider the matter, and meet me at the Consulate the next day with a definite answer."

During the next few days many meetings took place, but as the Government nearly always sent different chiefs to discuss matters, one had to go through the same process of explanation time after time. As each clause of the proposed agreement was read and explained it met with approval, but when asked to sign, they absolutely refused. Finally I cut down the clauses to two—the payment of one thousand dollars fine, and a written pledge for the safety of the Puletua chieftains still confined within the fence of the Consulate, and I gave them twenty-four hours in which to come to terms ; stating that if during that time no agreement were come to, I should hand the matter over to Captain Murray, asking him to enforce my demands. Captain Murray wrote to the Government, stating that if the matter was not satisfactorily settled by one p.m. on Monday, the 18th March, he would first of all destroy all Government property at Mulinuú, and if no settlement were then effected, he would proceed to destroy other villages and increase his demands. Some terrified white people came running to me to ask if we were going to bombard the town ; but I assured them that a box of lucifer matches would be all that was needful.

Of course I kept the German and American Consuls informed of the steps I had taken. This brought furious letters from Mr Griffin, who spread the wings of the American Eagle very wide indeed, and informed me that any action taken against the Samoans would be an insult to the United States. Mr Weber says he verily believes that Mr Griffin is periodically insane. At the request of the Government, Captain Murray gave them another day's grace, but they did not actually give in until the very last moment, when they saw that boats were manned and armed; then they came off to the *Sapphire* with the money, tied up in coloured handkerchiefs, consisting of a various assortment of coins ranging from French five-franc pieces to cast-iron Bolivian dollars. They also signed the pledge regarding the safety of the Puletua chiefs confined in the Consulate. The absurd part of it is that the Government, pleading great poverty (which is not true), spent the whole afternoon going from house to house in Apia begging assistance from the white residents in paying the fine; and almost every white trader, wishing to be on better terms with the natives than his neighbour, subscribed a few dollars, so that the beggars actually collected two or three hundred dollars before night, although I heard on good authority that they had got the thousand dollars together among themselves before they started on their begging expedition; and what confirms this is that when we came to count the money we found that they had brought some hundreds of dollars too much, which were of course returned to them, and they had a feast and a spree on the strength of it next day. The vaunted coming of the American man-of-war was merely a beach rumour, and these rumours were numerous ; perhaps the most amusing was that Sir Arthur Gordon had been carried off by the *Sapphire* as a prisoner to be tried in Fiji for stealing the Samoan schooner, *Elizabeth*. However, that rumour died out when the *Sapphire* returned to enforce the remainder of the fine.

The *Ada May*, the schooner in which Mamea, the native Ambassador, sailed for San Francisco, had now returned, but Mamea did not return in her. However, there was some account of the much-talked-of Treaty in the American papers. It appeared to be a very one-sided document, said nothing whatever about a Protectorate, but merely offered the good offices of the U.S. Government in any difficulties with foreigners.

As soon as the pledge was signed, I landed with a guard of Marines and marched the Puletua Chieftains from the Consulate (which they were very loth to leave), and saw that they had a fair start on their way home. However, I thought it best to remain in Samoa until Mamea's return and learn the truth about the American negotiations. So the *Sapphire* departed to Fiji without me.

TO MY SISTER.
                    BRITISH CONSULATE,
                         APIA.
                         4th April.

" Mrs Liardet and her family were still living at the Consulate when I arrived, and for three weeks I had to stop at an hotel, which was tolerably comfortable and clean, kept by a German, who had married Emma Coe, the handsome half-caste daughter of a former American Consul (see *South Sea Bubbles*, where Lord Pembroke said he put an accent on the é (Coe) to avoid scandal!) My office was, of course, in the Consulate, and I had about half a mile's walk to it through the town, which is something like Levuka, but more unpleasant. Most of the houses are grog shops, and there are plenty of loafing half-castes and natives hanging about them, and drunken rows of a night are by no means uncommon. There are, however, a few good houses. At the one end of the town is the establishment of Godefroy, the Hamburg merchants, a large substantial wooden building. The Manager, Mr Weber, is also German Consul and is inclined to be most friendly, assisting me in any way he can. And at the other end of the town is a somewhat similar establishment of Ruge and Heddeman, also Hamburg Merchants. These two firms do the greater part of the business of the place, and there are always several German vessels in the harbour. Towards Heddeman's house lives Dr Turner, Missionary and M.D., my most confidential acquaintance here, and a first-rate Samoan scholar. His house also is large and comfortable. The town consists of a straggling line of native and European houses running around the harbour, and the consulate is nearly in the middle of the line, anything but a pleasant situation, as there are grog shops on either side of it. Last Saturday Mrs Liardet left for Fiji, so I have now taken possession of the house. All the furniture (such as it was)

was sold. I have bought a few chairs and a table, etc., just enough to get along with, and set up house-keeping for myself. It is a six-roomed two-storied wooden house, very badly built, and was horribly dirty when I took possession, so I had to begin with a good scrub-down. I have engaged a Samoan (who speaks a little English) and his wife as servants, and my Fiji boy acts as cook. Altogether my house-keeping is a rather primitive arrangement, but it is quieter and more comfortable than the hotel. One great objection to the house is the want of good water. I have to send my boy over a mile for my drinking water, as I don't trust the stuff the people drink here. The hills do not rise abruptly from the sea as at Ovalau, but slope gradually back, so that all along the coast there is a good deal of level land. I can't tell you much about the natives yet, as I have not seen anything of them except those about the town, and I don't think it is fair to judge from them. The islands have been longer European-ized than Fiji, but I cannot say that the place seems more civilized. The so-called Government is merely a collection of chiefs of the successful side in the last war, and they know nothing and do nothing about governing. The people are such thieves that the small white planters have almost given up planting in despair, for the natives steal all the produce and kill and eat all the pigs and chickens; even the white missionaries have difficulties in keeping their things from them. Even when they are caught in the act of stealing, the Government will do nothing to punish the thieves, and I, of course, have continual disputes with them on the subject. In the chiefs I have to deal with I find an odd mixture of childishness and subtlety; personally, they are pleasant enough, and if they were not humbugged and bullied by rascally whites into being distrustful of everyone, I believe a good deal could be made of them. Several of them speak English tolerably well. The muchtalked-of American man-of-war has not yet made its appearance, and the Government refuse to do anything until their Ambassador returns.

"They were fully under the impression that America had granted them a Protectorate, but since the newspaper accounts of the treaty have arrived, and also since they have found out that the U.S. Consul cannot prevent England making demands and exacting payment for offences against British subjects, I think they have altered their minds. I don't think the natives are capable of setting up a good Government for themselves, and very much fear that they will again fall a prey to Yankee Adventurers. The Germans have by far the greatest interest in the group, and Godefroy has one large plantation under the management of an Englishman; with a large number of imported Polynesian labourers they employ it is possible to check to some extent the thieving of the natives. Everyone tells me that the natives are incorrigibly idle, and will never work as long as they can steal from white men, but I have so often heard the same statement from travellers elsewhere that I am not prepared to believe it until

I have seen something more of the people myself, although I own that I have too much fear of its proving true. It is curious that the natives here all live on the sea coast, and although the land amongst the hills is very good indeed, there is not a single village away from the beach.

" 5th April.—I spend my days in the Consulate trying to get the place into some order, and of course have frequent visits from planters and others, and when it gets cool I usually walk up to the river for a bathe, dine alone and go to bed early—not very exciting work !

" I forgot to tell you anything about the looks of the people. The men are not as a rule so fine looking as Fijians, but some of them are very handsome, and the old men especially look very dignified. The women I am disappointed in, some of them certainly are pretty, but they all have very gummy ankles, and are inclined to waddle rather than walk. They delight in bright colours, and use them with some taste. The houses I do not like at all ; a house consists of an oval thatch roof resting on slight-looking posts, *no walls at all !* When the wind or sun comes too strong from one quarter, they let down a sort of screen of plaited coconut leaves for shelter. The floors are made of small pebbles, with only a mat placed here and there to sit on. How they like to sleep on such hard floors with no padding of any sort under them I don't know. I don't think I shall care for it much, but I suppose I must try to-night for the first time, as I am off for a trip down the coast for a few days. I must say one thing in favour of the houses, that the work in the roof is sometimes beautiful—a sort of lattice-work made of bread-fruit tree wood and tied with sinnet."

To my sister—

" *April*, 1875.—I told you that you should have some account of my first trip into the country, and I am faithfully keeping my promise by sitting down to write to you the very night of my return. On Friday I was to have started in a canoe with Pilipopo, the Government chief of Manono, for that island, but the usual Polynesian delays made it five o'clock in the evening before we got off, as the canoe did not turn up, and I had to borrow a boat from a white store-keeper, and consequently missed the tide. My interpreter was Mataiasi, my own Samoan servant, whose English is *not* first-rate, but I am told that he is a very trustworthy fellow, and he swears by Great Britain and Malietoa (the king who is now out of power). Of Pilipopo I knew very little except that he was a member of the present Government (Taimua), but that Manono, his home, is the stronghold of the opposition party, and his affection for the present Government could not be supposed to be very strong. Manono is a small island at the west end of Upolu, and is the Bau of Samoa, the most aristocratic and influential village or district of these islands. We had a long pull before us, and did not expect to get to Manono until late at night ; my crew did as much talking as pulling, and as the conversation soon became political, it was rather hard work, with Mataiasi as interpreter, to answer all the questions in an intelligible way. I believe it was about three a.m. when we arrived at Manono, but I had no watch, and I had slept during a good part of the journey. Whenever I was sufficiently awake to hear the conversation I found them still hammering away at politics—Samoan politics, I mean; they never seem to get tired of discussing them. When we arrived, we walked into Pilipopo's house, no difficult matter as it has no walls. By degrees the different members of the family woke up, and said ' Talofa ' (How do you do ?). We made tea, had a smoke and a chat, and then went to bed, that is, stretched ourselves out on the mats where we were sitting. They gave me a good pile of mats, however (as I did not much care about the hard pebbly floor), and a roll of tappa for a pillow. The next morning about seven o'clock, after a bathe in the sea and a breakfast off lobster and yams, we started for Appolima, a small volcanic island about four miles from Manono. Pilipopo proposed that we should walk along the shore, and meet the boat at the starting place for Appolima. Manono is, I should say, about a mile in diameter and pretty nearly circular. Our walk took us about half round it, and the path ran along the seashore all the way. To look at the soil, one can hardly make out how anything grows at all, yet the island is a perfect garden of breadfruit, coco-nuts, bananas, papaws, and dracena, the latter grown for leaf dresses, but they boil and eat the root when food runs at all

short. In the centre of the island they grow a few
yams and some taro, but I did not see the plantations.
From the seashore to about thirty or forty yards
inland the soil appears to be nothing but white sand ;
but the coco-nut and breadfruit trees flourish on
it, and even some bananas. Inland the surface of
the soil is covered with black volcanic rocks and
stones, all the fruit-trees I have named growing
luxuriantly amongst them, and the soil is so porous
that not a single stream is to be seen running into the
sea, and I did not see a drop of water on the island.
I never had a wash in fresh water from Friday until
Monday, and lived on the demijohn of fresh water
I had luckily brought with me in the boat. They
tell me that there is a little bit of swamp inland on
which they grow their taro, and there is a small
supply of drinking water in the wet season ; but
this year being very dry, they have to send over to
Upolu for all the water they want for drinking and
cooking. All along the beach, under the shade of
the coco-nut trees, there are groups of houses, the
big family house in the centre, and a few poorer-
looking houses round. They keep the houses and
the surroundings very clean ; the floor of the houses,
as I told you, is made of small loose black stones
or coral, and there is an open space for bigger black
stones or sand for a few yards round every house,
never grass even where it would grow well.

"The natives live altogether in families, and the
family holds land in common ; each family elects
its own head, generally the eldest male of the best

blood, but they do not seem to be bound by any strong customary law in the matter of election, and pass over any one who does not please them. In Manono, where the land is thickly peopled, and there must be nearly a thousand inhabitants, it is divided off by walls of volcanic stone, but where the people are fewer, on the larger islands, this is not the case, and the boundaries, especially in the forest, are very vague, and will give much trouble when the land-purchases by white men come to be inquired into. And there will be the additional difficulty that the land has not always been sold by the head of the family, who alone appears entitled to deal with it; or the head of the family has sold it without the knowledge of his relations, and has not divided the purchase money amongst them, as he is bound by custom to do.

" The chiefs' families generally own a little more land than the others, but the chiefs themselves do not appear to have much definable power, although they possess a good deal of influence. All important questions were decided by a meeting of heads of families, until the formation of the present and late governments broke up some of the old customs, yet put nothing better in their place.

" Well, I have finished my walk as far as the passage in the reef where we were to start for Appolima, and I must go on with my day's journey. About three miles' row outside the reef brought us to Appolima, an island in almost every way different from Manono. It is, in fact, the crater of an extinct volcano, with precipitous sides towards the sea, in some parts about a thousand feet high. Where the cliff is lowest, there is one small break in the rim of the crater, the only landing place on the island. There is always a heavy swell in these seas, and the breakers were dashing splendidly against the black smooth cliffs as we rowed along to the passage. I had caught sight of this opening as we had passed by in the *Sapphire* on the way from Fiji, and knew what to expect. The break in the cliffs is about eighty yards wide, but this is blocked with big rocks over which the great rollers break and the white foam surges in the little basin inside. The passage itself through which the boat had to pass is not ten yards wide, and the seas almost break on to the ends of your oars. It was high tide, however; there was no wind, and my crew knew the way, so that there was not the slightest danger. You wait for a good wave, then give way together, and you are safely inside! The little basin would not do much more than hold my open boat when the tide was out, and in rough weather one might wait for weeks and not be able to get out again.

"There are about fifty acres of flat land in the centre of the crater, a few feet above the level of the sea; it then rises gently and gradually gets steeper and steeper until it reaches the almost knife-like ridge running round the island.

" The island is perfectly impregnable in war, and has always been important on that account. The only means of defence the inhabitants needed, was a strong rope which was passed across the narrow entrance and fastened into the cliffs on one side and lowered into the water just inside the passage. As a hostile canoe passed through, the rope was tightened, and the canoe upset.

" Everywhere, except the few acres of black stones and sand where the village of about twenty houses stands, breadfruit, coco-nuts and other fruit-trees grow even more luxuriously than on Manono ; there are a few fine ivi and other forest trees amongst them, and from the ridge about one hundred feet downwards there is a thick growth of wild wood. There is a sufficient drainage from the woodland to irrigate a few taro beds, and the water in the drinking pool looked clear and wholesome. But I could not face the village bathing hole, where the little stream ran out, or rather lost itself, on the beach, although I only had salt water to wash in in the morning.

"The chief of the place (it is allied to Manono, and considered to belong to it) presented me with a root of kava, and made pretty speeches, which I answered through Mataiasi : and after the young ladies of the place, who were rather nice-looking, had prepared it, we had a drink, smoked cigars, and then I got a native to show me the way up, and walked round the edge of the crater. The view from the top was good : one could look down on the thickly-wooded crater on the one side and on the sea breaking against the precipitous black rock on the other; and across the sea the mountains of Upolu or Savaii stretched away into the distance,

and the white breakers on the distant reef glistened
now and again in the sunlight. How my guide and
I managed to carry on a conversation I don't know,
as he could not speak English, but we talked away
quite happily and occasionally understood each
other, and he decked me with garlands of sweet-
scented leaves and scarlet hibiscus. The path was
not too good, and it took us about a couple of hours
to scramble all round the ridge, which was in some
places almost too sharp to walk along. Lunch was
ready when I came down, and after lunch we had a
long talk which, as usual, very soon became political,
whatever subject one started on. With the exception
of Pilipopo, whom I find to be rather unpopular in
his district on account of his connection with the
present government, the party were all, as Mataiasi
expressed it, for Malietoa and Great Britain. And
I am now beginning to see for myself what I have
often been told by the missionaries and others, that
the essence of native politics is to be found in the
' King Question ', that is, whether Malietoa or
Tupua shall be nominally King of all Samoa. Success
in either case would only be a triumph of family
pride, personal fitness for kingship having very little
to do with it. Malietoa himself behaved like a cur
during the last war, and deserted his party in the
most cowardly way, yet his claim to be King is not
much affected by his behaviour. Another uncomfortable element is that the Tupua family are Roman
Catholics, and the Malietoas Protestants, and ill-
feeling is added to the natural rivalry between the

two missions. After luncheon I clambered up on to the rocks and watched the rollers breaking into the passage, and saw the clever way the fragile-looking fishing canoes, holding only one man, were paddled in and out of the basin. Mataiasi had told me that he was going to have a swim, and I naturally thought that he intended to bathe inside the basin, but, much to my astonishment, I found him swimming about happily right amongst the breakers, every now and then lost from sight in the foam, but always avoiding the rocks, and apparently quite at his ease. It was no easy matter, however, when he wanted to get to shore again ; and he made several attempts before he could succeed in gaining the shore on the top of a big wave, and scrambling away before the next roller broke on him ; several times he touched the shore, but had to jump back again on the roller to avoid being dashed against the rocks. About five o'clock the water was high enough to get out through the passage. The Appolima chief made me a speech at parting, and expressed a hope of seeing me again, but added, that he hoped next time I would not bring Pilipopo with me, as that worthy in true native fashion had carried off a roast pig and a good store of cooked yams and bread-fruit, all of which, I expect, was meant for the Appolima people's Sunday dinner. We got to Manono about dark.

"On Sunday morning I walked right round Manono. There is nothing to add to what I told you before. The whole coast-line is thickly peopled.

In the afternoon I went to call on the French Priest, the only white man living on the island. He received me very cordially, and asked me to come to tea with him in the evening. He lives in a very very untidy fashion in a small unfurnished wooden house, altogether very uncomfortable-looking. The only pictures on the walls were a print of the heads of all the Popes, and a large brightly-coloured print of some dark-complexioned gentleman and ladies being roasted by some still darker-looking horned attendants, with a beautiful background of yellow and red flames. (This picture is evidently supplied to all the R.C. Missionaries: I have since seen it in other mission houses.) Notwithstanding his surroundings and the want of water at Manono, I liked what I saw of the father. He takes some interest in the natives, and insisted on my seeing the other high chiefs of the island before leaving, saying that Pilipopo was not popular, and did not represent the general feeling. I, of course, was only too glad to meet the other chiefs, and to have the benefit of the father's interpretation, so a message was sent, and the three leading chiefs came almost immediately. To my great surprise I had found the father strongly in favour of the Malietoa party, and most anxious for English protection or annexation, as he felt certain no native Government would ever be strong enough to keep order. Mataiasi, who came in soon after our conversation had begun, seemed suddenly to have become a great 'talking man', and held forth to the chiefs to such an extent that I had to ask the father what it was all about, as there was no checking him; the father, however, said that he was talking very sensibly (but I have to be very careful that he does not give out his own ideas as mine). Of course I have to answer many questions, and my general way out of a difficulty is to tell them what we do in Fiji in like cases; and I find this generally gives satisfaction. The people appear to feel that they are not strong enough by themselves, and wish for the protection of a strong power, and England is no doubt the favourite; but the people in office want to stick to their places, and think that, by getting a treaty with America and coquetting with other Governments, they may avoid their obligations and put off the day of reckoning with other countries, and still lead their own. They (the Government) cannot possibly do it. They are not strong enough to keep order, and every Consulate is full of complaints and claims for damages which they cannot satisfy; besides, they do not represent half their own country, and the other half is only waiting to get a chance of turning them out. Of course, they find whites who benefit by this state of things, and are always ready to persuade them that they are doing quite right, and advise them to reject all offers of assistance or attempts at compromise. My position is not an easy one. I preach conciliation and the formation of a strong native government, which all the best authorities tell me is an impossibility, and which I feel to be at least very unlikely myself. The chiefs seemed pleased with our meeting, and made many apologies for not being able to receive me in a suitable manner ; they wanted me to stay for a few days so that they might entertain me. This, however, I could not do, and I found that the real difficulty was that they were in the middle of a fono (council) with the Puletua chiefs, who were returning to Savaii. In the evening I went to tea with the Father, and then turned in early, as we were to start before dawn next day.

"About three thirty a.m. we had tea made, and then rowed over to Upolu, but had to wait for about half an hour for enough light to get right into the shore, during which time my crew had morning prayers and sang a sort of half-chant, half-hymn ; the singing was excellent. I was landed at daylight on the end of the island, and walked for about eight miles along the coast to Fasitotai. The native houses were more numerous than I expected. I stopped at the house of a white man at Mulifanua, thinking that it was the head station of Godefroy's large plantation. It was still quite early, and a good-looking young German came to receive me in his nightshirt, not expecting a visitor of my colour.

"Between this plantation and Fasitotai the destruction of the houses and property of the Puletua after the last war was painfully evident. Charred stumps, rotting logs, and old foundations of houses were to be seen all along the road. Some of the old coco-nut trees escaped, as it needed too much hard work to cut them down.

" I called at Mulifanua, the large plantation of Messrs. Godefroy, where there were nearly two thousand acres under cultivation, and the land claimed extends to nine thousand acres. That night I dined with Moipan, the Governor of the province, and Alipata, the chief Judge. The dinner was served on a table in European fashion, and was altogether very well arranged. Next day I received a visit from Sanga, and some of the Puletua chiefs who had been refugees in the Consulate, and had now returned to their homes. They are now living in wretched huts close to the sites of their old houses, which they are about to rebuild. I don't think, however, that they feel so sure of peace as to be induced to take too much trouble about erecting good houses, or even planting more food than is absolutely necessary."

Extracts from letters to Sir Arthur Gordon—
" The present Samoan Government are not strong, and their influence is decreasing. They have no doubt members from every district in Samoa, but these do not in the least represent the feelings of the people, and many of them are clinging to office because they are persons of no rank, and know that should the Government break up they would sink into obscurity again ; and they hang on to their offer to America as their last hope. No American man-of-war has arrived, and I am very doubtful whether Griffin has any real information that one is coming.

"Griffin is most anxious to get away. He is a man of no strength, and is merely a tool in the hands of others; he has no money, but is living on subscriptions from the natives, and is heartily sick of the place—I know this for certain. Griffin's failure to prevent the enforcement of the Barracouta fine, and his continual calls on the Government for money, have lost him all the influence he ever possessed. Weber is the real power in the place, but although the natives feel this and respect him, he is not popular with them, and they have no love for Germany. Weber is, of course, adverse to any foreign annexation, as Godefroys are doing a good business, and every year annexation is deferred gives them a better title to their lands. In the mean time they are very well able to take care of themselves, and if annexation cropped up, I have no doubt Weber would try and stop it; but I notice that he is taking great pains to settle his disputes with natives about land-titles and to survey his purchases.

. . . . .

"One would think that the present Government would try to conciliate, and would leave the King question alone, but all the best authorities tell me that they cannot leave it alone, and that it is sure to turn up soon, and that directly the Malietoa party get the upper hand, as they are bound to do, proposals for annexation will be offered.

. . . . .

"Now there is the other side of the question to look at; the country is in a most lawless state.

My few attempts to get justice done by inducing native judges to try native offenders against whites have been miserable failures.

"In one case the judge begged the accused out of friendship to himself to accept a judgment to pay a fine, and the accused walked out of the Court saying he would sooner die first, and has never paid a penny. In another case the Judge asked the accused if he had ever been told by the elders of his town that what he had done was wrong; this the accused admitted, and the Judge replied, ' Then I forgive you '.

"I have full reports of these cases, made by the natives themselves. The favourite mode of trial is ordeal by oath; they swear the whole of a neighbourhood to find out the perpetrator of a theft, that is, when one can wake them up to seeing about an offence at all. That there will be a disgraceful disturbance here some day soon, if the white landowners and planters do not get some protection against native thieves, I am quite sure.

"The Germans owning large estates have a number of imported (Line Island) labourers to protect them, and generally take the law into their own hands, and flog or paint with coal tar any native they catch stealing.

"Weber always talks about the Samoans requiring the whip and the sword for some years, and I am sure his rule would be a very severe one, if he got the chance of ruling them, and this in spite of his being a really kind-hearted man. But there is a want of sympathy between him and the Samoans, of which the latter appear to be very conscious.

SALCAILUA, SAVAII,
1878, *Easter Monday.*

" I have now come here to the west end of Savaii, in order to catch the *Active* which sails in a few days for Auckland with a cargo of copra ; I hope to induce the Captain to call at Fiji and take my letters, and I shall take the opportunity to investigate Cornwell's case—I mean the charge against him of ill-treating his labourers. I fear it is a very disgraceful affair altogether, and the Overseer, who appears to be a fiend, is not a British subject but an American, so unfortunately I cannot deal with him as Deputy Commissioner, and Griffin is not likely to move in the matter.

" The navigation of this south coast of Savaii is very dangerous in open boats. For thirty miles there is an iron-bound coast, with only two places where it is possible to run a boat into shore, and these passages are so bad that my crew refused to attempt them ; so (since the weather was threatening) I left my boat at Satapailea and walked here. The track is level but awfully rough, loose sharp volcanic rock crossed by roots of trees and overgrown with ferns. At the end of yesterday's walk, about twenty miles, my canvas shoes, which were new, were cut to pieces.

" In thirty miles I crossed only one stream, and that no larger than the Bureta river. There was

213

not another stream all along the coast. I don't see how much can ever be made of this part of the country. The villages are rather large, yet there is very little cultivation, but coco-nut and breadfruit trees are plentiful, and the natives are good fishermen.

.   .   .   .   .

" 24*th April.*—I had a hard day yesterday at Lata. Three men, seven children and eleven women have died since November. No doubt they were in a bad state when they arrived, but twenty-one deaths out of one hundred and thirty labourers is fearful. I will write you a full report as soon as I have my papers in order.

.   .   .   .   .

" I have fifteen miles' walk before me this afternoon, so I cannot write any more, only one thing I want to put clearly to you, that I only wish to stay here if I may try to bring about annexation—or rather, if I am not to throw cold water on any wish of the Samoans to become British, for it is useless to try and force annexation; but with very little encouragement it will, I think, be offered without any pressure on my part. I only want permission not to discourage it.[1]

.   .   .   .   .

The condition of the imported Tapituhea (Line Island) labourers at the plantation of Lata was appalling; unfortunately I have no copy of my

[1] This is the last letter I can find written from Samoa at this time.

report, which I believe was printed and circulated by the Colonial Office.

I arrived at Lata on Sunday afternoon, while the American Overseer was away, and walked round the plantation; to my surprise, I found that most of the labourers had already served some time in Fiji, and spoke Fijian. When the overseer returned and I told him I was going to hold an inquiry the next day, he raised no objection, and said, " I suppose you do not understand the Tapitehua language, and would like me to interpret for you ". I thanked him, and replied that as nearly all the labourers spoke Fijian, I should conduct the inquiry in that language and translate into English for his benefit. The estate had English owners, but the manager did not reside there, and the actual management was in the hands of the American Overseer, who was unbelievably callous to the sufferings of the labourers. Even the Samoans, who cordially dislike the Line Islanders, took pity on the poor wretches who fled from the plantation and were picked up nearly starving in the bush.

I well remember my long walk back to Satapailea, where I had left my boat. The first day I ran a point of rock into my shin, the next day the pain was considerable, and after walking all the morning by noon it was intense. There was nowhere to stop, and I only managed the last few miles with the help of one of my men supporting me under each arm. When we reached the Missionary's house I very nearly fainted on the doorstep, and

215   P

could have gone no further. The Missionary and his wife were hospitable, but it was some days before the inflammation had subsided sufficiently for me to be put in my boat and taken back to Apia, where Dr Turner soon patched me up.

" I remember the Missionary at Satapailea bewailing to me the difficulty of getting Samoans to work for him (especially in the matter of thatching his house, which needed attention every year), and the way the difficulty was finally overcome. A large pail of strong Epsom Salts and water was placed on the lawn in front of the house, and after a day's work each labourer was allowed to drink as much as he liked, and the supply of labourers never failed.

" At the end of ten weeks' stay in Samoa, during which time there had been no communication from Fiji, Mr Swanston arrived to relieve me, and I returned immediately to Fiji in the *Ondine*—six hundred miles in a twenty-ton cutter. Mr Houstoun came with me ; he had been in Samoa for some months, and had gained a great deal of useful information, which he always placed at my disposal. Sir Arthur was to start for England this month on leave of absence, and much wanted to see me before he left. M. des Voeux, whom I had met before in the West Indies, had already arrived in Fiji to act for Sir Arthur during his absence.

CHAPTER XVI

TONGA

After his visit to Samoa, Sir Arthur had sailed in H.M.S. *Sapphire* for Tonga, and arrived at Nukualofa on the 8th April.

The Tongan group of islands lie about two hundred miles to the south-east of Fiji, but some of the Fijian islands are nearer to Nukualofa, the capital of Tonga, than they are to Levuka, the capital of Fiji. Moreover, the inhabitants of the eastern part of the Fijian Archipelago are as much Tongan as Fijian in race, and many of the principal families of Tonga and Fiji are closely connected by inter-marriage and descent. Maafu, the Roko Tui Lau, the chief of the Eastern Islands of Fiji, was a Tongan of high birth, and a possible successor to the kingship of Tonga. Such being the conditions, it was natural that we should be interested in the Government and welfare of Tonga. All Tongans are Christians, and they have shewn a great desire to be recognized as a nation and to become Europeanized, and under the aegis of Mr Baker, the head of the Wesleyan Mission, they have become in a way Europeanized much too fast.

Sir Arthur had several interviews with the King, George Tubou, who received him in the most friendly way. Mr Baker was absent in New Zealand at the

time, and when Sir Arthur expressed his regret at
this to the King, the King replied that it was a good
thing, for had Mr Baker been present, he would
never have been allowed to have such pleasant and
instructive interviews with Sir Arthur.

Sir Arthur returned to Fiji convinced that the
Baker régime was not beneficial to Tonga, and that
it was unpopular with most of the Tongans. Without
giving Mr Baker away, the King let Sir Arthur know
that every effort had been made to prejudice him
against Sir Arthur himself, and against English
influence.

Sir Arthur was naturally alarmed at the fact that
the Germans had been granted the best harbour in
the group as a coaling station, and that for his service
in arranging this and for promoting the German
Treaty, Mr Baker had been given the Order of the
Red Eagle. Moreover, a German, Mr Sahl, who was
Imperial German Consul in Australia, had been
appointed Tongan Consul in Sydney. Mr Sahl was
also manager for Messrs Godefroys' firm in Australia,
as Mr Weber was in Samoa, and there was little
doubt that the object of Messrs Godefroy was to
obtain absolute control of the revenues and sole
direction of the Government of Tonga.

I remained only a fortnight in Fiji and then
sailed in the thirty-two-ton schooner *Louisiana* for
Tonga, as Deputy-Commissioner and Vice-Consul,
but as acting Consul-General during Sir Arthur's
absence on leave. It was a nine days' passage,
with calms and head winds. My companions were

Mr Wilkinson, our chief Interpreter and Native Commissioner in Fiji, Daniela Toa, a native parson, a Tongan by birth, and Mr Houstoun, who came on a visit. Wilkinson and Daniela could not be spared from Fiji for more than a few weeks. I also brought with me Ratu Epeli, a young Fijian Chief, and four or five native servants.

Extract from letter to my cousin—

Tonga,
July, 1898.

"I have been in Tonga more than a fortnight, and so can tell you a little about it. The country is dreadfully flat and uninteresting, that is, as much as I have seen of it, and I am told it is the same all over the Island. The town looks like a fifth-rate new Colonial watering-place; half a dozen or more wooden buildings face the shore, namely, the King's palace, courthouse, police barracks, printing office, bank, and some others, and at the back there are a number of very poor-looking native houses. King George, a dignified old gentleman, dressed in black, received me very graciously, and all the native swells have been very attentive. As I had no house to go to, the Government placed a large wooden storehouse at my disposal, and told their own carpenters and painters to do anything I wished. I set to work at once to make myself comfortable, and rather pride myself on the success of my efforts. The house is of the roughest weather-boarding, unlined, but I have matted the floors and walls, and have covered the rough furniture I have had made with stuff I brought with me. We are already quite a big household, and I have also written to a young friend of mine to join me from New Zealand, to stay with me and act as a sort of Secretary. Of Consular work there is really next to nothing to do, but the object of my coming is rather diplomatic than consular. Tonga is a united Government under the Sovereignty of King George Tubou, and, the Tongans being a quick, sharp-witted people, they have fancied that they could become changed from natives to Europeans all in a hurry, and are suffering from the consequences. The whole thing has been worked by the Missionaries, at the head of whom is a certain Mr Baker, a clever man of whom there are many stories, none much to his credit. The prevailing idea has been to turn all natives into white people by dressing them in European clothes, lodging them in European houses, and passing restrictive laws about the most harmless native industries, customs and amusements; in fact, the place is fearfully priest-ridden by the Wesleyan Ministers. The Government is on the latest ' civilized ' (?) principles, and there is a long Constitution Act, which the native authorities neither read nor understand ; indeed, half of it is written in English, and has never been translated into Tongan, and the principal work of the Government officers seems to be to exercise their newly-found authority by ' running in ' everybody for the most trifling offences, and by the present system of imprisonment creating criminals by the hundred. The greatest crime in Tonga, as far as I can make out by the laws, is murder, the next the making of native cloth (tapa)!!! an industry which we are doing our best to encourage in Fiji. There is very little doubt that Mr Baker is a trader in all but name, and that many of the laws have been passed to enable him to make money by importing goods from the colonies, nominally for Government or mission use. The mission contributions gathered from the people have been enormous, and have been extracted by the most unfair pressure. The worst of it is that nearly all the members of the Government are preachers and under strict church discipline, and any effort on my part to improve the laws will almost inevitably involve me in a row with the Church, which of course, I am anxious to avoid. Baker is secretly hated by some of the other Missionaries, and openly abused by some of them, but although he has been brought up several times before the Church (Wesleyan) Conference at Sydney, they have never been able to get the better of him. The natives have begun to find him out, and the feeling against him is beginning to be very strong indeed, but his influence in the Church, and the superstitious fear of doing anything against a Minister, prevents them from stirring. Through round-about ways the chiefs keep me supplied with full information of the latest Bakerian moves, and much to my amusement I find myself becoming the rallying-point of a Conservative reaction.

" At the King's orders about a hundred natives came to my house a few days ago, to sing mékés to me, and they sang the old songs of the land, which had not been heard for years. Baker, at a large Church meeting the next day, told them how Fiji was lost, given over utterly to sin and ruin, ruined even more politically and socially than morally, that the chiefs were now no more than common people, and why was this ? Because they had clung to the old songs of the land ! ! !

"At the same meeting he publicly reprimanded a native minister for coupling his (Baker's) name with that of a native minister in his prayers, telling him that the white Missionary should always be prayed for first and alone. This was all reported to me by the native Prime Minister the next day, of course on the understanding that I was not to divulge the name of the informer.

Baker only paid me a most formal visit on my arrival, which of course I returned, and he was profuse in his expressions of regard, and hoped that ' I would not make myself a stranger ', etc. But he never introduced me to his wife and family, which he has had good opportunities of doing, and has never really asked me to his house, so I thought the best thing was to ask him, so had him to dinner a few days ago, and we got on very well, although the man is undoubtedly a snob.

" The European clothes movement is most amusing. It is tabu to appear at the big church in native dress, and in consequence the miscellaneous collection of seedy black clothes and trousers is something wonderful. The ladies are resplendent in silks and satins, and tight lacing has lately come in fashion, but as the hill on which the church stands is steep (the only hillock in the island) and the ladies are not used to stays, a good deal of unlacing goes on when the service is over at the church doors. At a college examination which I attended a few days since, one of the lady spectators was dressed in a crimson satin dress sprigged with gold, a crimson and gold belt, a light blue silk and lace scarf, a hat much turned up at the sides, trimmed with purple satin and light blue ribbon and five pink and three dark red roses, and no shoes and stockings. During the performance I noticed that she got rid of the belt, and a good many hooks had come out of their eyes. Of course, when they get back to their own houses they take off all their European finery, get back into a native dress, sit in a draught to cool themselves, and naturally catch cold. A friend of mine, an English lady who keeps a small store here, had a conversation the other day with Miss Baker. ' Well ', she said, ' Miss Baker, have you seen the new Consul ? ' ' No.' ' Has he not been to call ? ' ' Yes, but Papa received him alone. I told Papa he might have asked him to luncheon, but I was told to be quiet and mind my own business.' ' But didn't you see him at the College yesterday ? ' ' Yes, he was there, but I was afraid to have a look at him.'

"If I could only get up a judicious flirtation with Miss Baker I might have it all my own way with the father, as I am sure a son-in-law must be very hard to find here.

" The native chiefs were rather shy about calling on me at first, but I let them know that I should be glad to see them, and all the native swells have now called, and I have had a great many of them to dine with me. They are very pleased, but cannot quite understand it. I, of course, treat them as I should any other gentlemen, and many of them are thorough gentlemen, and that is not what they are used to from Missionaries of the Baker type, or from the other white men here. The general decision arrived at is that it is a new thing, but decidedly ' vaka turaga '—chief-like.

" Well, you must be tired of Tongan tittle-tattle, but really the society here is most amusing ; the smaller the society the more the scandal ; and small-talk seems to be the rule all over the world."

To Sir A. Gordon.

14th July.

" David Unga, the Prime Minister, says that since my arrival all the low whites have kept so quiet that the police have very little work, and this pleases him immensely. I don't expect it will last. . . .

" The tabu on sulus (the native loin-cloth, about two yards of calico or native bark cloth wound around the waist and hanging to the knees) is almost at an end, except at the big church. The King himself walks about the town in a sulu in the daytime. I think the tabu on masi (native bark cloth) is nearly over too ; it is so unpopular.

"As there were many complaints about the amount of indebtedness to white traders by the natives, and the way the natives were being sold up under distress warrants from the native courts, I obtained permission from the King to hold an inquiry into the matter, and as many of the debts were on account of subscriptions to the Missionary Church I asked Mr Baker to join in the inquiry or to send a representative, but he declined having anything to do with it."

The method of collecting subscriptions for the Missionary Church was as follows—

The villagers were worked up into a state of excitement by means of Bo-Lotus, or night services, before the collection day, and when that day arrived Mr Baker would drive to the principal church of the district, having made arrangements with one of the agents of Godefroys' firm to be in attendance with a supply of money. This money the agent advanced to any native applying for a loan, the amount to be repaid in copra. Sometimes Mr Baker would himself advance the money to the trader, and receive an order on the firm of Godefroy for the amount.

The villagers would march round the church in procession, depositing silver in the plate each time they passed the altar, and see who could keep it up longest, village vieing with village, and individual with individual; and when their store was exhausted, in the heat of their excitement they would run out and borrow money from the trader, who had set up his table near the church door.

The following is one of the affidavits sworn before me by a trader—

" In the year 1872 I gave out money for the Missionary Collections, but not to a large amount. In 1874 I gave money to the natives at Kolovou, Kalogo, Afa and Hameliuli, Manuka, Navutoka, and Talafou. I went round these villages with Mr Baker to distribute to the natives on the day of collection for the Church. The money was given to me at the Ministers' houses, at the church door, and sometimes in the church itself. If I ran short of money, I called Mr Baker out of the church and asked him for more. I gave Mr Baker orders on the firm of Godefroy & Son, as I drew the money from him. I advanced about five thousand dollars ($5000) in the year 1875. Mr Baker several times advised me as to the safety of advancing money to certain individuals, about whom I had doubts of their ability to pay. I gave the money indiscriminately to anyone who applied for it. I took no receipts from the natives, merely wrote their names down in the book. Mr Payne, Mr Coventry and I, all advanced money at Mua.

" It was clearly understood, both by Mr Baker and the natives, that the advance was to be repaid in copra. There was considerable excitement at the time of the collections, Kerosene tins beating, and parties in the village vieing with each other in giving larger amounts. I collected some of these debts myself, but I left the firm of Godefroy before they were all collected."

(Signed)   P. S. BLOOMFIELD.

As the copra was entered in the accounts at much below its market price there was room for a large profit, in which we had a suspicion that Mr Baker shared, but of this of course we could get no proof. The result of this arrangement was that very many of the natives were in debt to the German firms, and under the new laws they were brought into court and distress warrants issued, if they could not pay, and they were sold up or had to give their labour to the Germans until the debt was liquidated. However, the German firms did not benefit as much as they expected, for as the copra crop had been short they were afraid to press the natives too hard, and they did not find the native labour much good to them. Two days after the inquiry it was reported to the Government that Mr Baker had himself satisfied the outstanding warrants for mission collecting debts to the amount of £300.

TO MY MOTHER.

July.

" The people are most anxious to build me a house on their side of the town, away from the white traders, and I think it would be a good move, and am thinking of buying a native-built Roman Catholic church (the Mission has just built a new

227

wooden one), and moving it to the spot chosen for me. It would make a splendid big house; the posts are first-rate, and the roof a very good one. Of course it would all have to be taken to pieces, as it measures 70 feet by 30 feet. Kitchen, servants' rooms, etc., would all be separate from the house itself.

"Mr Baker has been persuading the chiefs to live in little wooden shanties imported from New Zealand, so I was determined to live in a native house, which is much better suited to the climate, and to show that a native house built by the people themselves could be made both attractive and comfortable.

"The country is flat and very uninteresting. Nearly all the natives ride, but I have not bought a horse yet. However, yesterday I bought a small boat, a little tub of a dinghy, in which to go fishing. The climate is just simply splendid. I sleep under two blankets, and find it cold! The days are beautifully bright, and there is a strong trade-wind all day."

Extract from letter from Mr WILKINSON to SIR A. GORDON, *July*, 1878.

"Mr Maudslay gave a £5 prize for a (sailing) canoe Race. A Trial was made yesterday, which was a failure; but the race came off to-day very successfully, a Haapai canoe being the winner. Baker sent down word when he heard of the race, with orders that no preacher of any grade was to go in any of the canoes on pain of excommunication, which order was of course implicitly observed, much to the annoyance of the King, who highly approved of the affair."

To my Mother.

9th August.

" Away at the back of the town a Ladies' College is being built; the natives say they sigh whenever they pass by it. I don't wonder ; it must have cost no end of money, as it is built of Colonial hard wood timber, and the natives know that all the money comes out of their own mission subscriptions. Where the ladies are to come from, I don't know. All the chiefs to whom I have mentioned it vow that no daughters of theirs shall go there. The idea of educating in such a place girls who have afterwards to return to miserable little reed houses, to become the wives of natives, is too absurd. I was interrupted in my letter by a visit from 200 ladies, who have come to make me a present. They were all smartly dressed and decked with garlands, which they took off and threw down before me.

" The present of course consisted of eatables, yams, chickens, etc. They were the people from Mua, a town on the other side of the Island. Tungi, their chief, came with them, and he said all the women were very jealous of him, because they could not make a speech to me, and he could. That it was not his gift they were bringing, but a present (a thing of love and goodwill) which the women

229

themselves wanted to bring me. Then the usual civilities followed, and my talking man made a reply.

"Tungi is a man it does one good to look at ; he is so big and jolly and so full of fun, quite a chief of the old type, no new-fangled notions, but plenty of good sound sense, and most anxious to do good to his people and see them happy and comfortable."

To SIR A. GORDON.

8th August.

"Last night Tungi came to dine with me again, and we had a most interesting conversation. He told us a good deal about the Parliament, and everything seems going the right way. The smoking tabu is moderated, and when Tungi proposed the abolition of the Masi Tabu, and said, ' Don't let us talk about it. Let us sweep it away without another thought ', he tells me he thought they would bring down the house with applause. They shouted ' Tungi! Tungi!! We have a father among us yet! We are Tongans still, although we have hidden ourselves under whiteman's clothes '.

"We talked away last night for about three hours, and at last I apologized, and said that he must not go away with the notion that I wanted to lecture him on the things we were talking about. Tungi replied, ' Tell the Consul that is all humbug. He does lecture me, and it is the lectures we get here that have done us all so much good. I knew from the moment the Governor began to speak to us, that matters were on the mend ; he spoke to us of things we understood, and when they were things new to us, he put them in a way we could understand. And tell the Consul that good has been done in another way. This is the first Parliament that has been free from outside pressure. We talk about things like Tongans now, and don't have new things shoved down our throats '."

CHAPTER XVII

NIUAFU AND TONGA

In August the twenty-ton cutter *Orpheus* arrived from Fiji, to carry Wilkinson and Daniela back there; but as Wilkinson was not ready to start, I thought it a good opportunity to make a trip to Niuafu, which I knew to be one of Baker's pet hunting grounds.

It is a small volcanic island about 300 miles to the north of Tongatapu—equidistant from Samoa and Fiji. Captain Cocks, our harbour master in Fiji, was in charge of the *Orpheus*, which had been borrowed from a Fijian Chief with a scratch native crew. I asked him if he had a chronometer, and he said no, but he had an old watch which went pretty well! However, he did possess a sextant, and said he thought he could find Niuafu all right. Cocks is a dismal person unless there is any danger, and then he becomes quite cheerful; but no one in the Pacific can handle a cutter better, or find his way more safely among coral reefs. We hit off Niuafu all right, and when approaching the land several natives swam off a long distance to meet us. There is no anchorage and no regular landing-place, so I had to jump on shore from the dinghy between waves.

For the thirty hours I spent on shore Cocks kept off and on, within signalling distance. I went through the usual reception from the chiefs, and was buried under garlands from the women. The chiefs were loud in complaint of Missionary rule. All the males over sixteen pay taxes, and there are only 300 tax-payers, but the Mission manages to squeeze $10,000 to $12,000 a year out of them in Mission subscriptions, which is paid in copra at trade price, so there is room for profit; money is given as well, and the people pay all building expenses for church, schools, and teacher's houses. There were two white traders living on the Island, agents for Godefroy and Hede-mann, and both confirmed what the chiefs told me, and said that great pressure was put upon the natives to subscribe more than they really could afford.

I climbed up to the ridge of the crater and looked down on the lake which filled the depression. The Island grows the largest coco-nuts in the Pacific.[1]

Before leaving, the chief asked me if I would give him a passage to Nukualofa. To this I agreed, but knowing the ways of natives I bargained that he should not bring more than two followers. When we got back to the *Orpheus* we were running away with a good breeze and a free sheet when Cocks came to me and said, " We have a number of persons on board ". " Only the chief and his two attendants whom I brought off with me." I replied. " Why, Sir ", he said, " the hold is full of them, and there

[1] The Island measures three and a half miles by three miles. All the villages were destroyed in the Eruption in 1886.

are two women among them." I had them all brought aft, and true enough found we were twenty-two on board all told !

I began to give the Chief a bit of my mind, but he said at once that he knew nothing about it, and it appeared that the men and women had swum off, and while Cocks was dozing at the helm had climbed on board and dropped down into the hold. What was to be done ? The chief had no hesitation; he said, " Throw them all overboard, they will swim ashore all right ". But by this time we were some miles from land, and strong swimmers as I knew the Tongans to be, I dared not do it.

We had only enough food and water for ourselves, and the outlook was not pleasant. There was a strong breeze, and as I was tired I turned in early, but about midnight was on deck again almost before my eyes were open, with the sudden jar. Cocks, who had hardly ever left the helm since we left Nukualofa, was really tired out, and had put a native at the helm, himself lying down near him on the deck, and I suppose the helmsman was half alseep. The cutter had jibed, all standing, and the main sheet in flying over had knocked the helmsman on the head, and he was lying bleeding on the deck. By sheer good luck nothing carried away, for, as Cocks told me quite cheerfully, it was a good thing I had never examined the step of the mast, for it was quite rotten, and he could run his penknife into it anywhere. As soon as we got things straight, I insisted on Cocks having a sleep, saying that though no sailor

I could keep a course, if he would give it me; and I promised not to jibe her. None of the natives could be trusted. We were five days getting back to Nukualofa, and arrived with absolutely no food left, having been many hours becalmed near the uninhabited volcano of Kau, which rises abruptly from the sea to a height of three thousand three hundred and eighty feet.

To SIR A. GORDON,

8th September.

" I have enclosed a copy of a letter I have written to the Wesleyan Committee in Sydney. I think it is the only course to pursue, as I shall come into open collision with Baker before long, and before I have time to receive any answer from you. It is war to the knife; the letter gives you some fresh information, and in addition you may take it for granted that all you have heard here is true. He is so much hated by the natives, and so untrustworthy, that it would be impossible for us to work together.

" *30th Sept.*—Of course the clearest proof and most damaging case against Baker is the large number of debts for missionary subscriptions which have been brought before the native courts and the amounts recovered by distress, and it was this clear proof which made me write as I did to the Committee. There were still a number of debts owing, and some distress warrants had been issued, but the inquiry I was making frightened Baker, and he paid up the money himself to satisfy them."

To my MOTHER.

" *3rd Sept.*, '78.—Everything goes on quietly and slowly here, and there is very little to write about. Frank Symonds, a man whose acquaintance I made in New Zealand, has accepted an offer I made him to come and live with me, and he arrived about three weeks ago. I like him much, and am very glad indeed that he has come, as I should be very lonely when Wilkinson returns to Fiji, which he will most likely do next week. Mr Houstoun left a fortnight ago for Samoa, where I expect he will remain, as he likes political rows, and Samoa is quite topsy-turvy just now. A German and an American man-of-war are in Apia Harbour, and I think matters must come to a crisis soon.

" Here, the native parliament is still sitting, as the King says, ' Eating yams and talking nonsense '. The weather has become very changeable, and the natives feel the effects of the changes very much. I am besieged for medicine, and have to go a regular round of visits to see patients every day. There is an epidemic of whooping cough, for which I can do little, but the children are dreadfully pulled down by it, and are suffering from dysentery. Luckily, I have a good store of native arrowroot, which came to me as my share of a mangeti (native feast) in Fiji, and I have plenty of Brand's beef-tea, and these do wonders. It is a scarce time for native food in the Islands."

To SIR A. GORDON.

" 30*th* Sept., '78.—The Treaty which I have been instructed to negotiate with the Government is at last signed, and I send it to you by this mail. The King asked me to strike out the Steamer Clause, and I did so. I gave every possible opportunity of discussion and explanation, and I really believe that there is not a word in it that is not thoroughly well understood, and the King is evidently delighted both with the Treaty itself and with the manner in which it has been submitted to him. He says this time it is 'Sava Sava'. The last clause was inserted at his own request. I do hope that I shall soon get an answer to my despatch, which will show him that the completion of the Treaty will not be long delayed. I hear that nearly all the measures I have recommended have been or very soon will be passed by the Parliament.

" *Nov.*, '78.—I have just returned from a week's visit to Mua, a town twelve miles distant, on the other side of the lagoon. I like it much better than Nukualofa. It is the old capital and the home of the Tui Tongas, the sacred kings of Tonga. Their descendants still live there, but they have fallen from their high estate and been deprived of their titles.

" I spent a day or two clearing the undergrowth away from the ancient tombs of the Tui Tongas, built of huge stones. Many of the stones were brought in canoes from the Island of Uvea (Wallis Island), about 500 miles to the north. I wish the Tongans were as numerous, and had as much go in them in these days. The canoes must have been of great size, for the story is undoubtedly true, and the Uveans show the quarries they were taken from. One stone I measured was 24 feet by 10 feet, and it was not the heaviest. The tombs are all hidden in the bush, and the natives themselves know very little about them ; huge Ficus and Casuarina trees are growing among them. I managed to interest Gara-ni-valu (="spoiling for a fight"), a descendant of the Tui Tongas (with a Fijian name), in the tombs of his ancestors, and we spent the day clearing the scrub from one of them. I have got the chief to promise that when the yam planting is over we will have a feast, and turn out the whole village, and clear them properly. I found twelve tombs, some with one tier, others with two, three, four, and five tiers of stones.

" There is a well known Trilithon Hahake, about eight miles from Mua."

Housekeeping was not an easy matter at Nukualofa. A few chickens, a little fish and some yams could be bought, but we were often hard put to it for food. When an occasional trading schooner called, we always rowed off to her to see what we could secure. If she came from New Zealand, we could sometimes get a bag of onions or a cheese, and if from San Francisco, some tins of asparagus ; but we often drew a blank. I must now record a curious coincidence. Among the stores I had from home were six small jars of Maille's French Mustard, and on the day when the last of our stores was consumed, and the last spoonful had been scraped from the mustard-pot, a schooner appeared in sight. Frank Symonds asked me if he should row off to her, and I said it was hardly worth while, since we had drawn so many blanks lately. "However", he replied, "I think I will try." As he shoved off, he called out, "What shall I bring you back?" and I cried, "Six jars of Maille's French Mustard." I might as well have asked for the moon. When he returned I said, "What luck, Frank?" and he replied, "Six jars of Maille's French Mustard." I thought he was joking, but there were the jars sure enough. Frank told me that when he rowed alongside the schooner the skipper called out, "What can I do for you, sir?" and Frank answered, "Sell me six jars of Maille's French Mustard". "All right", said the skipper, "come aboard", and, diving into his cabin, he produced the six jars, and told Frank that about two years earlier a Frenchman in Samoa had asked him to procure them from Auckland, when he returned to New Zealand, or to order them from Sydney, and that he had managed to procure them; but when next he returned to Samoa, the Frenchman was dead, and he had carried them about the Pacific for a couple of years, and was glad to get rid of them.

The new cases from Fortnum & Mason's arrived on Christmas Eve, just in time for me to be able to give a good dinner to the homeless Britishers in Nukualofa on Christmas Day. Then I started on a trip to the Haapai group, in a five-ton cutter, and had the very nearest shave of being wrecked on the Hafaiva Reef in the night, during a terrific squall that struck us suddenly and broke the boom. Luckily, my half-caste pilot was very skilful, and we spliced the broken boom with two oars, and just managed to get enough sail on her to claw off ; but the roaring of the reef in the dark was too close to be pleasant.

To SIR A. GORDON—

" 29*th* *Jan.*, '79.—I believed for a long time that the Sydney people were right in disbelieving in any definite agency by Baker for Godefroy's firm, but Mr Hanslip, my interpreter, who was for some time employed by that firm, assures me he saw a draft of an agreement between Weber and Baker, the exact terms of which he is not able to remember, but that it was much of the same nature as the Steinburger Agreement ; that Baker was to use his influence with the Government for the advantage of the firm, especially in the matter of inducing them to levy a money and not a produce tax, and that he was to receive 10s. per ton commission on all produce which, by his management, was sold to the firm (as for instance on all the produce bought by the native traders with money loaned by the Bank, which was invariably transferred to the firm). Baker made some (slight) alterations in the draft, and Mr Hanslip did not see the agreement after it was signed, but was told by Mr Troud (Godefroy's manager) that its terms were accepted.

"Of course I cannot make any use of this information. That Mr Baker received the commission on copra brought to the firm through his agency Mr Hanslip has no doubt whatever. Apart from disapproving such an agreement, Mr Hanslip, who is a thoroughly honest man, was very sore on the matter, since he received, as manager in Tonga, only 5s. a ton on produce which passed through his hands in the usual course of trade. The knowledge of such an agreement having existed makes me very suspicious in other cases where Baker's honesty may be called in question.

"The worst news is about the Secretaryship to the King. As you know, I suggested Mr Troud to fill the place, and the King appeared to approve highly of the idea. When Weber was here (he came in a German man-of-war) he regularly jumped the claim, and persuaded the King to accept someone on trial *selected by the Emperor of Germany*. Baker acted as interpreter, and certainly did not dissent, and from the King's account to me, appears to have thrown his interest on Weber's side. I heard nothing of this until just before Christmas, when the King let it out on my making some allusion to his employing Troud. The King told me it was his mind to ask Troud to be secretary, but that he did not like to refuse Weber and Baker, who had explained that it was a mistake for him to have a man who *was too much of a chief*, and that a man from Germany would want such a small salary.

"It is a very monotonous life, our principal occupation is house building. The house I am now living in is miserable during wet weather, mosquitoes swarm, as it is built half over a swamp, and as there are no glass windows it is necessary to put up the shutters when it rains, which makes it hot and dark.

"I found that it would cost £300 to build a three-roomed wooden cottage without offices, fencing or furniture. A native house will, in the long run, cost as much; but instead of one of the miserable cottages the chiefs here live in, I shall have a really comfortable house and surroundings. The situation is not quite what I should have chosen, but it was the wish of the King and of the governing chiefs that I should live near them, so I made no objection.

"I bought the old Roman Catholic church at Mafanga and made arrangements with David Unga for the prison labourers to move and rebuild it at a certain price. The work is being tolerably well done, as the King takes a good deal of interest in it. All the European carpentering we are doing ourselves, that is we have put up about 300 yards of good picket fencing, and have nearly finished building a wooden kitchen and store-room, 20 feet by 10 feet, which is roofed with iron for the sake of the drinking water. Hanslip is a very fair carpenter, and directs our building operations, and I find the work keeps us in good health without the necessity of going long lonely walks along these very dull roads. I hope to finish the new Consulate without giving a day's work to a professional carpenter."

The old church had four splendid great greenheart posts, which we scraped and polished, supporting the usual cross-beams. All the crossings of the beams and of the narrow rafters of the bird-cagelike roof were tied with sinnet (cocoa-nut fibre string) of three colours worked into elaborate patterns, which were most effective ; for the King had sent all the old native craftsmen to do it skilfully.

The floor of the old church (70 feet by 30 feet) had been laid in blue gum timber from Australia, and we had the greatest difficulty in relaying it, for it had been down for fifty years, and was as hard as iron, and every nail-hole had to be drilled, as no nail could be driven through it. The walls of the new house were of crossed reeds, Tongan fashion, and the ten glass doors I imported from New Zealand. The inner lining was of reeds, each panel worked in a different pattern with coloured sinnet. A reed screen cut off the two opposite ends of the house, one forming the office, and the other the diningroom.

The bedrooms were separate native houses. Mine was a gem. When out riding one day near Mua, I had taken refuge from a storm in what was used as a cart-shed ; but on looking up into the roof I beheld the best native roof I had ever seen. I then learned that a " Tui Tonga fifine " that is, a woman of the sacred Tongan family, had died in the house some years before, and the house had to be abandoned. The narrow rafters and crosspieces, instead of being as usual of coconut wood, were made of green-heart, and I further learned that, many years before, a large war canoe had come over on a friendly visit from Fiji, and according to custom had been presented to the Tui Tonga ; but as the Tongans did not make use of such canoes it had been cut up into thin strips, and this roof built of the timber. I promptly bought the house, removed the thatch and had the roof carried in four pieces to the Consulate, where the roof was retied by the experts, and the house erected.

Then came the difficulty of finding a good lining for the reed walls. There was a mangrove swamp near the shore about two miles away, and I experimented with the long aerial roots of the mangroves. They answered the purpose splendidly. When cut up and the bark peeled off them, sand-papered and oiled, they looked like rods of old ivory, and after some search I collected enough, each about six feet long, to panel the whole room, each panel being worked with a different pattern in coloured sinnet.

The Roman Catholics had been some years collecting money to build their new church, and I believe it has cost them about £3,000. Most of the work was done by lay brothers. It was a wooden building of great size, with a galvanized iron roof.

A huge log of Kauri pine, which had been washed ashore and must have come from New Zealand, was used as a pedestal for a statue of the Virgin, and

MY HOUSE IN TONGA.

stood between the two wooden towers. I attended
the consecration ceremony. The day before I had
made a wooden cross about three feet high, and
in the morning had completely covered it with the
blooms of the splendid double crimson hibiscus,
and hung a wreath of white gardenias over the arms.
I managed to get some white satin ribbon to cover
the pole, and sent the cross to the padres, who were
delighted with it, and it was carried by an acolyte
at the head of the procession.

To SIR A. GORDON—

" 25th Jan., '79.—I had told the King some time
ago that, as I was well aware how many wild reports
were in circulation, I should always be glad to give
him the fullest information about any of my doings.
Some days afterwards, when we had been drinking
kava together, I noticed that he sent all his people
away when the faikava was over, and when we were
alone he asked me if I could tell him what I had
written about to Sydney, and what I was doing
about Mission matters. I assented, and we met by
appointment again that afternoon. In the mean time
I wrote out some notes for my interpreter, and when
we met I gave the King a consecutive account of
all I had done in the matter, including the account
of your interview with the Wesleyan Ministers in
Sydney. No one knows better than the King the
dodges Baker has been up to, to prevent my gaining
any influence. He listened most attentively to the

account I gave him, and thanked me very much for putting the matter clearly before him; before leaving he turned to my interpreter, and said that he did not wish to pay me compliments, but that he could not sufficiently admire the patience with which I had done my work under the treatment I had received, and that he felt sure that had it been in other hands it would speedily have ended in a very unpleasant quarrel (I believe the expression was stronger and better put in Tongan, but much to that effect).

"The resolutions passed by Parliament about engaging a doctor have come to nothing. I have spoken to the King on the subject, but nothing definite can be got out of him. He, however, admitted the truth of what Baker always denies, that it was owing to Baker's advice that the attempt to engage a doctor two years ago was frustrated."

King George Tubou was already an old man, having been born in 1797.

I asked him one day if he remembered Mariner, and he said yes. Mariner's story [1] is told in Dr Martin's book. Mariner was clerk to the Captain of the 500-ton Privateer *Port au Prince*, which, after a successful privateering voyage in the Eastern Pacific, went whaling. After filling up with oil she sprang a bad leak, and in 1806 drifted across the Pacific badly waterlogged to the Haapai group of the Tonga Islands, where the crew mutinied and insisted on

[1] *An Account of the Natives of the Tonga Islands.* John Murray, 1818.

landing, when they were all killed by the natives. The Tongans seized the ship, and in their anxiety to secure iron knocked the hoop-iron off the oil barrels, so that the oil burst out to the depth of two feet above the water in the hold, and eight of the natives were smothered, for although they could swim in the water below they could not swim up through the oil. The King (who was then a boy of ten) told me he was pulled out of the oil by some of his attendants, and that they called Mariner "Toki" (an iron axe), because they got their first iron axes from the *Port au Prince*. Mariner's life was saved, because the sailors had treated him with some consideration, and the Tongans thought he must be the son of a chief, and he lived for four years in the Islands.

CHAPTER XVIII

SAMOA, TONGA AND HOME

Feb., 1879.—In February I received, with despatches from the Foreign Office, a letter from Mr Gorrie, the Chief Justice of Fiji, to say he had been able to send H.M.S. Schooner *Sandfly* to Tonga to bring me back to Fiji, if I could leave my district, as M. des Voeux was very short-handed, and in urgent need of my services. So I left Frank Symonds in charge of the Consulate, and sailed in H.M.S. *Sandfly*, 150-ton naval schooner, for Fiji, and arrived at Levuka on the 20th February, after enduring a terrific gale which lasted five days, and was probably the tail of the hurricane which did so much damage in Tonga. On arrival I received a telegram posted from Sydney, giving me the sad news of my mother's death. I stayed at Nasova with the des Voeuxs, returning to my old work. We made one trip in H.M.S. *Cormorant* under command of my very old friend, Captain James Bruce, to Vanua Levu, to attend the funeral of Tui Thakau, which was carried out with full native honours; and Jimmy Bruce landed all his men and contributed much to the ceremony.

In May I returned in the 30-ton Schooner *Louisiana* to Tonga: ten days' passage with head winds and calms. On my arrival at Nukualofa I was shocked to see the amount of damage done by the hurricane. The large wooden warehouse, which I had made my home since arriving in Tonga the year before, had totally disappeared, only the posts which had supported the floor-joists marked the spot where it had stood. Two hundred native houses had been blown down, and the New Roman Catholic church had also disappeared; nothing but foundation posts and the huge Kauri Pine Log which had supported the statue of the Virgin were to be seen, and some of the sheets of corrugated iron from the roof had been found a mile inland.

My new house had almost entirely escaped damage. I had been careful to cover the thatch on the roof with large meshed wire netting, and had stayed this netting and the side posts with wire cables to large stones buried in the ground, about six or eight feet from the sides of the house. These precautions proved quite successful, and luckily I had moved all my belongings from the old house before leaving for Fiji.

The thatch roof is the danger to native houses, and it was a common thing in Fiji, on the threat of a hurricane, to see the population of a village sitting on the roofs of their houses endeavouring to keep the thatch down; for if the wind turned up the thatch and got inside the house was doomed.

Letter to my sister—

VAVAU,
16th June.

" I had brought back with me from Fiji a good many plants for my garden, coloured crotons from the Solomon Islands, cuttings which I had struck when in Fiji ; and I had also received wardian cases with plants I had ordered from Sydney and from Singapore, so my garden was well started. An orange hedge had been planted inside the picket fence.

" Then, much to my disgust, I received a telegram from Lord Salisbury (sent to Auckland, New Zealand, and brought on in a schooner which had been cruising about for some time before reaching Tonga), ordering me to go at once to Samoa, where disturbances were expected. I don't want to go a little bit, as I have my house to finish, and a good many things to do in Tonga ; but go I must, and am now on my way. I left Tonga about a week ago in a trading schooner of fifty tons, with a cabin about as big as your dining-room table, with six other passengers, including one woman and two children. Just a little bit crowded ! Piles of timber, and a huge boat for one of the traders, blocked up the decks ; and our diet was salt horse and hard tack. Luckily, it has been fine weather, and my fellow passengers were very civil and cheery, so I did not mind it much, but I do need a vessel of my own very much indeed. We were two days at Haapai, and then came on here, to Vavau, the northern island of the Tongan group. I am now staying with the Missionary, and am quite on my best behaviour, but it is just a little bit dull at the Mission House, and I don't think I will try it again, if I can help it.

" The House is quite new, and cost the Mission £1,500. So you see the hardship of a missionary's life is not likely to be very great, when the Mission can afford to pay such a price for a house for the Missionary to live in. This Missionary, Mr Minus, hates his brother parson, Mr Baker, with quite a Christian hatred, so we have someone to abuse in common, which affords us a good deal of satisfaction.

" The King's grandson, Wellington Gu, is the governor of this island, and is the most civilized of natives, speaks good English, plays the harmonium, and reads music, dresses like a white man, but is a dreadful snob. I don't think he is really a bad fellow, but much patting on the back by Baker and German men-of-war has turned his head. He took me for a ride in his buggy with a pair of horses, and I went to dinner with him yesterday evening."

MISSION HOUSE,
APIA, SAMOA.
27th June, '79.

" I came on here in the schooner *Oavalau*, 140 tons, new and quite comfortable. (Our only trouble was carrying away our triatic stay in a strong wind, when it looked for a few moments as though we should lose our foremast, but the Captain was at the helm, and soon had her up in the wind, and matters were put right.)

" Another Mission House, but quite a different affair. Dr Turner is an old friend of mine, and he is not a Wesleyan, which is a comfort.

" Politics here are very mixed, and I am keeping quiet, biding my time. I don't think it will come to fighting, but it is impossible to make sure of anything. A German man-of-war, the *Bismark*, is in harbour, and an American, the *Lackawana*, arrived yesterday. I wish she had kept away, as she will only complicate matters. I am not expecting an English vessel, and don't want one, although every one here seems to think I ought to carry a man-of-war in my pocket. I suppose I must stay here until something is settled. I tried to hire a house, but there is not one to be had; the hotel is horrid, and I am glad to take refuge here. Swanston, the English Consul, has no room for me at the Consulate, and I should not care to stay with him if he had. Dr Turner is about the best Samoan scholar in the Islands, which is a great help to me, and he appears to be delighted to have me here."

Apia had been taken over as a neutral district by the foreign Consuls, and I as Consul-General had to take the Chair at our meetings, and was faced by Weber, the German Consul, the American Consul, commonly known as Dismal Jimmy, the Captain of the German man-of-war, and the British Consul, Mr Swanston (whom I did not trust), and a little later, if I remember right, by a second German Captain. I had rather a difficult position, for I was under thirty, a good deal younger than the rest of them. However, Captain Chandler, the American, was an old dear; he saw that I was in rather a tight place, and did all he could to back me up. Dismal Jimmy never made a suggestion, but he objected to everything; however, I found out his weak spot. I drafted all the proclamations and notices, etc., which we agreed upon, but they never satisfied Dismal Jimmy, unless they were allowed to be altered into his rather peculiar English. So they were all re-submitted to him, and as long as the sense was the same we allowed him to have his way, and his satisfied pride was most comic, and things went smoothly.

As men-of-war were so much in evidence, I was delighted when, in August, H.M.S. *Cormorant* at last turned up. Jimmy Bruce had not in the least expected to find me here, and his reception and his feigned regret that he could not do me proper honour, as his was not a saluting ship, were most amusing. He brought the news that Sir Arthur Gordon was on his way out across the Pacific, and that the mail steamer was to call at Pango-Pango, where the *Cormorant* was to meet him. I believe Sir Arthur found, when he arrived in England, that he had no power to appoint me Acting-Consul-General without consulting the Foreign Office, but I never heard a word from the Foreign Office on the subject, and as Lord Salisbury had ordered me to take charge in Samoa, where a British Consul was already stationed, and my name was afterwards included in the full powers for concluding treaties, I can only suppose the F.O. acquiesced in my acting appointment.

The German and American ships both gave me a twelve-gun salute when I paid my official visits.

18th *August*, '79.—About the 18th August I sailed in H.M.S. *Cormorant* for Pango-Pango, the beautiful harbour in the Island of Tutuila, and on the 20th the mail steamer from San Francisco arrived off the port to transfer Sir Arthur, and Captain Knollys and Victor Williamson to the *Cormorant*.

That afternoon I presented to Sir Arthur a document signed by all the principal Samoan Chiefs, offering the Cession of Samoa to Great Britain, which had been handed to me just before I left Apia for Pango-Pango; and my disappointment was great when told that it could not be accepted on account of some arrangement that had been come to between the English and German Governments in the matter, and that I must hand the document back to the Chiefs and inform the other Consuls of what I had done.

The next day we returned to Apia. Sir Arthur stayed at the Consulate, where Mr Graves had been installed for some time in Swanston's Place. I stayed on with Dr and Mrs Turner, where I was most comfortable. The first few days were taken up with official visits. Then there was a general meeting of Consuls and naval Captains, English, German and American, when it was arranged to acknowledge Malietoa as King of Samoa, as his party were now completely in the ascendant, and were in possession of Malinuú, which was looked on as the headquarters of Government.

The next day all of us foreign officials and captains went to Mulinuú point, where Malietoa and all the principal chiefs were assembled. Just as we were arriving, old Sanga, one of the chiefs whom I had freed from his refuge in the Consulate the year before, caught sight of me, and insisted on embracing me and rubbing noses. Luckily, I was able to dodge behind a coco-nut tree, and I don't think the other foreigners witnessed the performance. Then after speeches from Sir Arthur and Malietoa, there was a ceremonial kava drinking, and Malietoa was drunk in as King of Samoa. Then we adjourned to an arbour of palm branches hung with garlands of flowers, where we sat on the ground and were given an excellent native feast, all most admirably done. All the natives were in their smartest native costumes, with exquisitely fine mats for sulus. These are their most treasured possessions, and are handed down for generations. I had held one for some time, given me as a pledge for the good behaviour of the inhabitants of the Island of Tuituila. It was very old and most carefully patched, and although of good size I could easily have pulled it through a napkin ring. The women too were all in native costume of bright colours, but all harmoniously blended.

The next day, at the Consulate, the articles of a treaty were discussed and agreed to, and were taken to the King for his approval. The day following the Treaty was signed by Sir Arthur and myself, and the two plenipotentiaries chosen by the King in due form. The next few days were occupied with meetings of the Foreign Consuls discussing the convention for the municipal Government of Apia and the neutral district.

While this was going on, on the 30th August, Malietoa and fourteen high chiefs called on Sir

Arthur at the Consulate, and offered a formal and unconditional Cession of Samoa to Great Britain. This had again to be refused, and Sir Arthur explained to them that as they had already concluded agreements with Germany and the United States, it was impossible for him to accept the Cession, but that he would bring the matter before the British Government.

Malietoa then said that by the arrangement of a municipality in Apia and the neutral territory, the Samoans had already shewn that they could not rule themselves, and they now desired the protection of one of the great powers for the Government of all Samoa ; and that he would write a letter to the Queen and to the German Emperor and the President of the United States saying that they could not cede Samoa to three powers, and that they preferred to cede to Great Britain.

As the Treaty was now signed, and the convention for the Municipal Government agreed to, on the 4th September we all sailed in the *Cormorant* for Tonga, arriving at Nukualofa on the 7th September, 1879. As the *Cormorant* was under orders to return immediately to New Zealand, Sir Arthur could only stay twenty-four hours, long enough to enable the King to agree to the extension of the Agreement I had made with him until a definite treaty could be negotiated, and the *Cormorant* then sailed to land Sir Arthur and his staff in Fiji.

Things went on quietly in Tonga for a month. Then on the 4th October the Wesleyan Mission ship

John Wesley arrived with the Rev. B. Chapman, the Chairman of the Wesleyan Board of Missions in Australia, and the Rev. Clark on board. These gentlemen called on me, and stated that they had been appointed by the Wesleyan Conference to inquire into the charges I had made against Mr Baker, and requested me to produce my proofs. I replied that they were endeavouring to place me in a most unfair position. That a year had elapsed since I had made those charges, and they had taken no steps in the matter, and had done nothing; that they knew as well as I did that all Tongans were under the Church discipline, and all those who had given me information had been subject to ecclesiastical censure, and practically excommunicated by Mr Baker; that there was little chance of my being able to get them to repeat what they told me, and that I thought it was for them to make such inquiries into Mr Baker's conduct as seemed to them fit. After a good deal of conversation they said that they had come two thousand miles on purpose to hold this investigation, and that they must beg of me to do what I could to clear up matters. So I gave in, and the investigation took place in my house and lasted three weeks, I acting as a sort of counsel for the prosecution. Baker put up a hard fight, but I got much more than I expected out of the cross-examination of his witnesses, and left quite confident that I had proved my case. At the end of the three weeks I was quite done up, and was glad to ask the commissioners for their decision. However, to my astonishment they told me that they were not empowered to give any decision, but must report the matter back to the Australian Conference.

It was a beautiful moonlight night, and I walked along the beach for an hour or two with Mr Chapman, and told him very clearly what I thought of the procedure, but I could not move him, although finally he told me that both he and Mr Clark were quite satisfied with what I had done, and with what I had been able to show them. And with that I had to be contented.

A week or so later Mr Baker left for New Zealand, and on the 23rd November Sir Arthur arrived in the H.M.S. *Emerald*. The following week was occupied in negotiations of a Treaty with Tonga, which was signed by Sir Arthur Gordon and myself on the 29th. Then as I badly needed a change, I asked for leave of absence and returned in the *Emerald* to Fiji. In the beginning of 1880 I sailed for Sydney, where I stayed at the Colonial Club, and thus ended my connection with the South Seas.

To Sir Arthur Gordon—

SYDNEY,
15*th February*, 1880.

" My stay in Sydney has been considerably longer than I anticipated. The very day after my arrival I was laid up with an abcess in my knee, and confined to bed for a fortnight. I am all right again now, and intend to sail by P. & O. steamer for Calcutta on Tuesday. My brother and sister have, I learn, been in India for about a month, and I expect to meet them in Calcutta.

" The Baker business has ended as might have been expected. The conference spent many days over it, and then decided that Baker should not go back to Tonga as a Missionary. He refused a Colonial appointment from them, and takes a year's rest as a Supernumerary, during which time he will pay a visit to Tonga, to take back Unga's body (the King's son who had died in New Zealand) and to collect materials for a book on Tonga and a biography of King George Tubou. Although not a Missionary Baker will still be a Wesleyan Minister, and as such can preach, etc., if asked to do so by the local minister ; and with the influence we know he exercises over Watkin, it will be odd if he does not persuade the Tongans that he has been completely triumphant. I cannot believe that Baker returns to Tonga with those objects which he professes to have in view. He wrote a pamphlet giving his side of the case, which Chapman tells me was most emphatically condemned on every point by the Conference. Chapman and Clark would gladly have kept Baker out of Tonga altogether, but were apparently frightened to put pressure on the Conference, Chapman telling me that it would have done more harm to the Mission if Baker had been forbidden to return, and had then ignored the prohibition ! They evidently expect that he will give them trouble, but are frightened to do anything to prevent it, Chapman ending his conversation with the usual

ex/ression of his strong conviction that Providence
will not let the Mission cause suffer through the
actions of one man like Baker. I am afraid he would
be shocked if I called it ' trusting to luck '.

" *Postscript.*—The luck was certainly against them,
for Baker returned from New Zealand to Tonga in
a German man-of-war bringing Unga's body with
him, and then persuaded the King to appoint him
Prime Minister in Unga's place. He then threw off
all connection with the Wesleyan Mission, and set
up the Free Church of Tonga, and Mr Watkin joined
him."

This idea of a free and independent Church tickled
the vanity of the Tongans, and the majority joined
it, and there followed years of strife between the
Wesleyans and the Free. However, Baker's persecu-
tion of the Wesleyans was so outrageous that finally
some of the sufferers made an attempt on his life.
It was not successful, but his son and daughter, who
were with him at the time, were both wounded.
On this followed executions, imprisonment, floggings,
and exile for many of the unfortunate Wesleyans ;
and Baker even sought to connect a Wesleyan Missionary and the English Vice-Consul with the crime.
But it was not until 1890 that Baker's tyranny became
so atrocious that Sir John Thurston visited Tonga
in an English man-of-war, and under his powers as
High Commissioner for the Western Pacific removed
Baker, and forbad him to return to the Islands.

Then at the King's request Mr (now Sir) Basil

Thomson was sent from Fiji to assist in straightening out the affairs of the Tongan Government. He has published a most interesting and amusing account of his experiences in a book entitled, *The Diversions of a Prime Minister*. King George Tubou died in February, 1893, in his ninety-seventh year, having been born in 1797.

A British Protectorate over the Tongan Islands was proclaimed in 1900.

When I arrived in England, finding that Sir Arthur Gordon was not going to remain in Fiji, and had accepted the Government of New Zealand, I intimated my desire to resign my appointments and retire from Government Service, and thereupon received the following letters :—

From the Colonial Office—

" I am to convey to you the permission you desire, with an expression of Lord Kimberley's regret that the High Commission will no longer have the advantage of your services, which have been of much value."

From the Foreign Office—

" I am to express to you the thanks of Her Majesty's Government for your very efficient services, which have met with the entire approval of Her Majesty's Government."